D1195584

Ethical Issues in Behavior Modification

REPORT OF THE
AMERICAN PSYCHOLOGICAL
ASSOCIATION COMMISSION

Stephanie B. Stolz
and Associates

Foreword by Albert Bandura

Members of the Commission

Sidney W. Bijou, Chair
Jerome Frank
Paul R. Friedman
James G. Holland
Leonard Krasner
Hugh Lacey
Stephanie B. Stolz
David Wexler
G. Terence Wilson

Ethical Issues in Behavior Modification

Jossey-Bass Publishers
San Francisco • Washington • London • 1978

ETHICAL ISSUES IN BEHAVIOR MODIFICATION
Report of the American Psychological Association Commission
by Stephanie B. Stolz and Associates

Copyright © 1978 by: Jossey-Bass, Inc., Publishers
433 California Street
San Francisco, California 94104
&
Jossey-Bass Limited
28 Banner Street
London EC1Y 8QE

Copyright under International, Pan American, and Universal Copyright Conventions. All rights reserved. No part of this book may be reproduced in any form—except for brief quotation (not to exceed 1,000 words) in a review or professional work—without permission in writing from the publishers.

Library of Congress Catalogue Card Number LC 78-52233

International Standard Book Number ISBN 0-87589-368-6

Manufactured in the United States of America

JACKET DESIGN BY WILLI BAUM

FIRST EDITION

Code 7809

616.891
St69e

The Jossey-Bass Social and
Behavioral Science Series

3830822

Foreword

During the past two decades, the knowledge and means of behavior influence have grown dramatically. Widely publicized reports—some thoughtful, some grossly exaggerated, and some misinformed—about these recent developments have aroused considerable public concern over the uses to which psychological knowledge is put. As the means of personal and social change continue to increase in effectiveness, their potential use for human betterment and harm becomes much greater.

A responsible social science must concern itself not only with advancement of knowledge but also with the social consequences of its applications. In keeping with its commitment to this dual responsibility, the American Psychological Association formed a commission representing different disciplines to examine the ethical and legal issues in the modification of human behavior. Serving as arbiter of ethical matters is no easy task. We owe a considerable debt of gratitude to the members of this commission for preparing one of the most thoughtful statements on the ethics of behavior modification. No other volume so clearly analyzes the philosophical, ethical, and legal issues involved in the exercise of human influence in diverse social settings.

Foreword

In utilizing behavioral methods for remedial purposes, one must distinguish between social regulation and treatment. Social regulation subordinates the interest of the individual to the group, prescribes conduct by institutional means, and authorizes coercive measures to force compliance; and agents of social regulation work mainly to further institutional goals. In the case of treatment, the interests of the individual are given priority, personal consent and choice about direction of change are possible, the right to terminate the relationship is recognized, and the agent of change works mainly for the benefit of the individual seeking help.

A psychological technology operates within the values, ideologies, and power structures of a social system. It is in institutional rather than in personal applications that the value premises of psychological practices become most controversial. Ethical dilemmas arise repeatedly when practitioners bear the double responsibility of furthering institutional goals while at the same time attempting to serve diverse individual interests. When these aims do not coincide, questions arise about whether the individuals or the institutional practices require change. The direction in which such value dilemmas are resolved rests partly on how much power the various constituencies exercise in determining the functions and practices of social institutions. Recognizing the broader social obligations of behavior scientists, the authors of this volume rightfully devote major attention to the institutional applications of behavioral principles.

On close examination, the value and ethical issues are not as unique to practices labeled *behavioral* as it is commonly made to appear. There are certain principal ways in which people can influence each other's feelings, thoughts, and behavior. The major challenge is how to assure that this growing knowledge is put to service for human betterment. This thoughtful book makes a substantial contribution toward this end.

Stanford, California
January 1978

ALBERT BANDURA
David Starr Jordan Professor of Social Sciences in Psychology, Stanford University

Preface

On February 14, 1974, the Law Enforcement Assistance Administration (LEAA) announced that it was banning further use of anticrime funds for behavior modification programs in prisons. In a news release the following day, the American Psychological Association (APA) called for "an evaluation of the use and misuse of behavior modification procedures in the criminal justice system." The association's statement noted that

> Behavior modification involves a large number of procedures, some of which are clearly abhorrent to psychologists as well as to the public. Other procedures, however, are humane, benign, systematic, educational, and effective. Psychologists have been in the forefront in developing and improving such procedures and applying them. The banning of these procedures will result in a regression to outmoded, unsystematic forms of inhumanity in prisons that have characterized society's past treatment of its criminal offenders.

> The LEAA action, in equating all behavior modification with the *Clockwork Orange* type of aversive conditioning, thus results in an injustice to the public and to prison inmates. The LEAA action will tend to stifle the development of humane forms of treatment that provide the offender the opportunity to fully realize his or her potential as a contributing member of society. The APA urges a reconsideration of the valuable educational methods of behavior change and, at the same time, the development of procedures to protect the rights of inmates against arbitrary and misguided forms of treatment.

The Board of Social and Ethical Responsibility of the APA, at its meeting on March 7 and 8, 1974, expressed concern that the news release did not properly reflect a reasoned consensus of APA opinion. Consequently, the board asked APA President Albert Bandura and the board of directors to form a task force on the use and misuse of behavior modification techniques. The board also suggested that the task force include representatives of other professions concerned with this area.

On March 22, 1974, Albert Bandura invited members of the board of directors to respond expeditiously to the growing public and professional concern in the area of behavior modification and to name prospective members to a task force on behavior modification. Following consultation with members of the central office staff, Bandura appointed a task force representing the professions of psychology, psychiatry, law, and philosophy, including persons reflecting diverse viewpoints within the field of behavior modification.

Members of the Commission

Shortly after its formation, the task force was "upgraded" to the status of an APA commission. The members of the commission were

- Sidney W. Bijou of the University of Illinois, Urbana-Champaign, a psychologist who pioneered efforts to use behavior modification techniques with normal and deviant children
- Jerome Frank, who is both a psychologist and a psychiatrist, pro-

fessor emeritus from the Johns Hopkins University, and one representative of a nonbehavioral point of view

- Paul R. Friedman, an attorney and director of the Mental Health Law Project, Washington, D.C., one of the legal experts on the commission
- James G. Holland of the Learning Research and Development Center of the University of Pittsburgh, a psychologist and behavior modification researcher who has been critical of the application of behavior modification in prison settings
- Leonard Krasner, a psychologist from the State University of New York at Stony Brook, a contributor to major classic historical reviews of the area of behavior modification and then a member of the APA board of directors
- Hugh Lacey, of Swarthmore College, a philosopher who provided a broader perspective on the ethical issues involved in the application of behavior modification
- Stephanie B. Stolz, a psychologist from the National Institute of Mental Health (NIMH), a past member of the American Psychiatric Association Task Force on Behavior Therapy, concomitantly involved in various activities at NIMH related to the ethics of behavior modification, and a member of committees of the Association for the Advancement of Behavior Therapy dealing with the issues of standards for behavior modification
- David Wexler of the School of Law at the University of Arizona, who wrote a major legal critique on the use of token economies with mental patients
- G. Terence Wilson, of the Graduate School of Applied and Professional Psychology at Rutgers University, a psychologist, teacher, and practitioner whose work is associated with a social learning conceptualization of behavior modification

Initially, Nicholas Hobbs, provost of Vanderbilt University and author of a recent major report on children for the secretary of the Department of Health, Education, and Welfare, had agreed to join the commission, but obligations abroad precluded his continued participation. The Consumers Union had been invited to participate in the commission, but was unable to spare a knowledgeable staff member. Unfortunately, an appropriate consumer representative who was a former prisoner could not be located either. The commission decided that it would operate on the assumption that the nonpsychologist members, particularly the attorneys, would serve to balance the interests from within and outside of psychology.

The commission was staffed by APA Policy Studies Officer Serena Stier, a clinical psychologist who had previously specialized in family and group therapy at the University of California at Los Angeles Neuropsychiatric Institute and at the California School of Professional Psychology. Sidney W. Bijou agreed to serve as the chairperson of the commission.

Operation of the Commission

The initial organizational meeting of the commission was held July 12, 1974. Additional meetings of the full commission were held on October 10 and 11, 1974; February 13 and 14, 1975; June 2 and 3, 1975; October 2 and 3, 1975; and February 12 and 13, 1976. For each of these meetings, the agenda book included readings focusing on the ethical, legal, and social concerns involved in behavior modification.

Initially, the commission had to struggle with clarifying its mission, because the area is a vast and complicated one, and no specific direction was given by the board of directors. The mission statement eventually developed by the commission is as follows: "The Commission on Behavior Modification will focus on the area of applied behavior analysis in research and practice in order to recommend effective courses of action to deal with the legal, ethical, and professional issues raised by these behavior-influencing procedures."

The commission decided to gather appropriate information through a case-study method. This method involved the selection of major settings in which behavior modification is applied and the evaluation of how behavior modification operates in these settings, in terms of the following issues:

1. *Who is the client?* What is the process of identifying the client and consequently of determining to whom the therapist is responsible?

2. *How are the goals of therapy set?* Who defines the problem? What means are available for monitoring and redefining the problem?
3. *How is the initial form of treatment selected?* To what extent are alternative treatments available? Who weighs the benefits and risks of a particular treatment? How is the adequacy of a treatment determined? What methods are developed for maintaining the efficacy of a treatment outside the therapy?
4. *How is the confidentiality of the client protected?* What methods of record keeping exist?
5. *How is the quality of treatment assured?* To whom are the therapist and the therapeutic facility accountable?
6. *What protection mechanisms exist?* What is done about informed consent, consensual agreement, contractual agreements, offering other alternatives, or monitoring results? In what way is the competence of the therapist monitored?
7. *How are the concerns of research and therapy balanced?*

   In order to gather information firsthand, the commission set up task forces to explore the use of behavior modification in various settings. The following task forces were created: (1) outpatient settings—Frank; (2) community mental health centers—Bijou, Holland, Krasner, Stolz, and Wexler; (3) mental institutions—Frank, Friedman, Stolz, and Wexler; (4) institutions for the retarded—Bijou and Wexler; (5) schools—Krasner and Wilson; and (6) prisons—Holland and Lacey.

Each of these task forces either visited one or more typical settings or read extensive detailed descriptions of programs conducted in typical settings. Applying the case-study method, the task forces evaluated the extent to which the setting being studied elucidated the potential legal, ethical, and social problems with respect to behavior modification. The task force considering institutions for the retarded drew on the experience of the special task force to the state of Florida for the development of guidelines for the use of behavior modification in institutions for the retarded; the membership of the commission's task force in that area overlapped with that of the Florida task force. Some of the task forces and their subcommittees met separately from the commission as a whole in order to complete their analyses. Subcommittees of the task forces submitted reports on their case studies.

In addition, the commission invited various individuals to its meetings in order to review the activities of other groups concerned with behavior modification. Most of the commission meetings were attended by a member of the central office staff of the American Psychiatric Association. In addition, the commission shared its work with other relevant groups within the American Psychological Association, such as the Task Force on Privacy and Confidentiality and the Task Force on Model Criteria Sets involved in developing guidelines for peer review. The commission also met with a representative from the staff of the National Commission for the Protection of Human Subjects of Biomedical and Behavioral Research.

Members of the commission prepared papers and participated in the Conference on the Issues Raised by the Application of Behavior Modification in Closed Institutions, held in June 1975, under the auspices of the Behavioral Law Center of the Institute for Behavioral Research, Silver Spring, Maryland. Commission members also participated in various conferences throughout the country, including the meeting of the American Orthopsychiatric Association in 1975 (Gittelman, 1975). The commission itself presented a report on the issues raised by the case studies to the membership of the American Psychological Association at the 1975 convention in Chicago (Bijou, 1975) and discussed its recommendations in an open meeting at the 1976 APA convention in Washington, D.C. (Bijou, 1976), as well as at the 1976 convention of the Association for Advancement of Behavior Therapy in New York City (Frank, 1976). Furthermore, commission staff, during the existence of the commission, were in communication with press representatives, members of the APA, and members of the general public concerned with the area of behavior modification.

Instead of developing a restrictive set of guidelines for the use of behavior modification, the commission decided that its final report should address the issues involved in the application of behavior modification to particular settings. An initial draft report was prepared in June 1976 and was circulated for comment to individuals within and outside the association who had expressed an interest and concern in this area. A second draft, responding to these comments and including the commission's own reconsideration of the initial draft, was also circulated. The commission then prepared a final report for presentation to the APA council of representatives in August 1977. Stolz coordinated this effort and was the editor of the report. The APA Board of Professional Affairs recommended "with enthusiasm" at its October 1977 meeting that the report be published. The report of the APA Commission on Behavior Modification is not an official publication of APA.

January 1978

American Psychological Association Commission on Behavior Modification

Contents

	Foreword *Albert Bandura*	ix
	Preface	xi
	The Author	xxi
One	Behavior Modification in Context	1
Two	Ethics of Interventions: The Major Issues	17
Three	Out-Patient Settings	35
Four	Institutions	41
Five	Schools	47

Six	Prisons	59
Seven	A Critique of the Use of Behavior Modification in Prisons	73
Eight	Society	91
Nine	Recommendations	101
	Ethical Standards of Psychologists: 1977 Revision	115
	Standards for Providers of Psychological Services	133
	Ethical and Legal Issues Related to Psychological Interventions: A Selected Annotated Bibliography *Stephanie B. Stolz*	165
	References	183
	Index	195

The Author

STEPHANIE B. STOLZ is director of the Division of Alcoholism, Drug Abuse, and Mental Health in the Department of Health, Education, and Welfare Regional Office in Kansas City, a position she took in 1977. Her interest in the ethical aspects of behavior modification developed in connection with a conference held in 1974 on professional issues in behavior modification organized by W. Scott Wood at Drake University.

Stolz earned her B.A. degree in psychology (1959) at Reed College and her master's degree in psychology (1961) at the University of Washington. She received her Ph.D. degree in animal experimental psychology and physiological psychology at the University of Washington in 1963. She was trained in behavior modification while on a U.S. Public Health Service postdoctoral fellowship at the University of Kansas Department of Human Development in 1966–1967, where she worked with Donald M. Baer and Montrose M. Wolf.

The Author

After several years as Director of Research at the National Children's Center in Washington, D.C. (1967–1970), Stolz worked for nearly eight years as Chief of the Small Grants Section at the National Institute of Mental Health, Rockville, Maryland. Following her participation in the Drake University conference, she participated in other conferences on ethics and published numerous papers and chapters on the topic. In addition to her 1974 membership appointment to the American Psychological Association Commission on Behavior Modification, she was a member of the American Psychiatric Association Task Force on Behavior Therapy (1971–1973) and participated in the committee that developed the Association for Advancement of Behavior Therapy's list of Ethical Issues for Human Services. Stolz was the major author of the policy recommendations on the ethics of behavior modification for the National Institute of Mental Health.

Stolz is a Fellow of the American Psychological Association and serves as a member of the National Advisory Board of *est,* an educational corporation. She has been secretary-treasurer of the Association for Advancement of Behavior Therapy (1974–1977), and president of the Society for the Experimental Analysis of Behavior and chairman of its board of directors (1975–1977). She married Donald M. Baer in 1977; they live in Lawrence, Kansas.

Ethical Issues in Behavior Modification

REPORT OF THE
AMERICAN PSYCHOLOGICAL
ASSOCIATION COMMISSION

ONE

Behavior Modification in Context

Behavioral technology is spreading rapidly through schools, clinic practice, mental hospitals, institutions for the mentally retarded, prisons, homes, army basic training, vocational and industrial settings, and social planning. Variously called *behavior modification, behavior therapy, applied behavior analysis, contingency management,* and *conditioning therapy,* practice in this field involves the use of principles of behavior in the deliberate alteration of human behavior. The act of controlling others' behavior (or attempting to do so) has enmeshed behavioral professionals deeply in social, political, and ethical issues. How and by whom are problems to be defined and goals set? Does the psychologist serve established power structures in modifying an individual's behavior, or is the psychologist obligated primarily (or exclusively) to the interests of the person whose behavior is being changed? Can the psychologist ethically serve both the power structure and the target individual? To enable us to examine these and other issues, behavior change programs in a variety of settings are explored in this book.

Ethics and Interventions

Although this book is restricted specifically to behavior modification, it is important to note that the issues discussed here are relevant to all types of psychological interventions, even to psychological assessment. Ethical issues such as who has the right to label, influence, control, or manipulate another person, under what circumstances, and for what goals are inherent in all interventions. The bulk of this book is directed toward behavior modification, as the commission was charged to do by the American Psychological Association. We have, however, directed our final recommendations to all kinds of psychological interventions, because it would be inappropriate and unrealistic to restrict them to one of the many kinds of procedures designed to influence behavior. Rather, these concerns should be shared and heeded by all concerned with changing human behavior.

Behavior Modification and Some Definitions

Behavior modification and the other terms used to describe this field refer to a specific approach to dealing with human behavior. Investigators in this field do not agree as to the single most appropriate term for the field. Of all the terms, the two most widely used are *behavior modification* and *behavior therapy.* The term *behavior therapy* tends to carry a connotation of clinical interventions that use techniques derived from a wide range of areas in experimental psychology, especially from classical conditioning; *behavior modification* tends to connote applications of operant conditioning principles to socially significant problems in both normal and deviant populations in a wide range of settings. Another term sometimes used, *applied behavior analysis,* primarily describes the use of operant conditioning principles in nonclinical settings. These terms will be used interchangeably in this report.

Not only is there a lack of consensus on the best name for the field, but there is also no agreement among investigators in this area as to a single, simple definition of *behavior modification,* and different authors propose different definitions. However, in the large and continually growing professional, research, and popular literature on behavior modification, the various definitions overlap considerably. They generally link behavior modification with the broad field of psychology through the use of concepts and principles, derived from experimental and social psychology, for changing human behavior; they generally mention an emphasis on the measurement of behavior in its natural setting; some of the definitions focus on specific techniques used by practitioners. Despite this variety of interpretations, enough elements are common to warrant a single generic label, *behavior modification.*

Rather than attempting still one more definition of behavior modification, we will list some characteristics that are shared by the work of many investigators and practitioners in this field. Enough differences exist that there is probably no investigator whose practice can be characterized by all the factors listed. Rather, the practice of behavior modification and behavior therapy is likely to be characterized by some, even if not all, of the following:

1. Behavior modification practice involves measuring the occurrence of the behavior to be changed and of the desired behavior; many persons believe that the emphasis on measurement is the distinguishing hallmark of behavior modification.
2. In behavior modification, problems are analyzed in terms of what people do and do not do. Psychodynamic and personality trait labels are generally not used to describe people and their problems.
3. Behavior modification is based on a model of human behavior that assumes that human behavior follows natural laws and that people's behavior, whether viewed as normal and usual or deviant and unusual, is an adaptation to their circumstances. Be-

havior labeled as abnormal, antisocial, or deviant is considered to reflect the interactions of individuals with their environment and is not viewed as necessarily symptomatic of some underlying pathology.

4. Because abnormal behavior is considered to be learned and maintained in the same manner as normal behavior, behavior modification holds that behavior labeled as abnormal can be changed or modified directly, through the application of learning principles, rather than indirectly, by treating presumed underlying personality dynamics. Even when troublesome behavior has a suspected physiological etiology, it may be amenable to a learning-based intervention, so that some modification is possible through changes in the relation between individuals and their environments.
5. Ideally, the goals of a behavorial intervention are selected in the context of an initial functional analysis or assessment of the problem behavior. The question is posed as to what the determinants, maintainers, and consequences of current behavior are and what possible alternatives could be developed.
6. This analysis is based, whenever possible, on observations of the client in the setting where the problem behavior occurs. The observations may be made by the client, a peer of the client, or the psychologist. To the extent possible, the observations are quantified.
7. Behavior modification practice entails an explicit specification of conditions under which behavior will be changed and a plan for the objective evaluation of the outcome of the change effort, including measurement of the behavior's occurrence.
8. Behavior modification is a diverse field, and behavioral techniques comprise a family of quite different methods. Most behavorial techniques are based on the principles of classical and operant conditioning. Some behavioral professionals restrict themselves to environmental manipulations; others give causal status to cognitive factors and other private events, emphasize cognitive mediation and vicarious and symbolic learning processes, like modeling, or use drugs as an adjunct to the therapy.

9. Although appropriate background and training are needed for the persons planning and supervising behavior modification programs, the interventions themselves can often be effected by paraprofessionals or other individuals without extensive or formal training, such as parents or peers of the persons whose behavior is to be changed, as well as by the target individuals themselves.

Techniques Used in Behavior Modification

Because this book is directed to a consideration of the ethical issues raised by behavior modification, we do not feel that a detailed description of specific behavior modification techniques is appropriate. Rather, our book will assume that the reader has some familiarity with such techniques as shaping, desensitization, token economies, and modeling. Many books are now available that describe the technology of behavior modification (see, for example, Bootzin, 1975; Gelfand and Hartmann, 1975; Kazdin, 1975; O'Leary and O'Leary, 1972; Sherman, 1973).

What Behavior Modification Is Not

Professionals in this field agree that behavior modification does not include psychosurgery, electroconvulsive therapy, or the noncontingent administration of drugs—that is, the administration of drugs independent of any specific behavior of the person receiving the medication. Such procedures do modify behavior, but that does not make them *behavior modification techniques* in the sense that we will be using the term in this book.

Historical Context of Behavior Modification

Although behavior modification in its modern sense came into prominence in the psychological literature only in the 1950s, this general approach to human behavior can be traced to the origins of the science of psychology in the latter part of the nineteenth century. Behavior modification can be seen as the most recent manifestation of the broad philosophy and methodology of behaviorism.

This book is not the place for a comprehensive review of the history of behavior modification. We will only touch on some of the most important antecedents to the development of the field. Major influences, after Pavlov, Thorndike, and Watson, were the research and theoretical writings of Kantor (1969) and Skinner (1938, 1953, 1957, 1961, 1968, 1969) in experimental psychology, Wolpe (1958, 1968, 1969a, 1969b, 1969c) in psychiatry, Bijou and Baer (1961) in developmental psychology, and the publications of the group of investigators working at the Maudsley Hospital in London, England, under the auspices of Eysenck (for example, see 1960, 1964). Other key influences on behavior modification came from clinical and social psychology (for example, see Dollard and Miller, 1950).

Historical Context of Ethical Concerns*

Just as behavior modification has grown out of an empirical and behavioral approach to human behavior, so general concerns about the ethics of psychologists and of behavior modification programs have developed from more general concerns with the ethics of medical practice and of research with humans.

Since the end of World War II and the discovery of the atrocities committed by the scientists working for the Nazis, physicians and others whose activities involve humans have come under increasing control and regulation. The civil rights movement and, more recently, a series of court cases concerned with issues such as the right to privacy and the right to effective treatment have further focused attention on individuals' rights and on scientific and therapeutic activities involving humans. Concurrently, the rights of human participants in research have been expanded and clarified (Katz, 1972).

* Some of the material in this and subsequent sections is based on Stolz (in press, a).

International Codes

Initial regulations applied only to medical research. These included the Nuremberg Code (Bernstein, 1975), the Declaration of Helsinki (World Medical Association, 1964), and a statement by Britain's Medical Research Council (1964). These codes provide for the voluntary consent of the subject and for a balance of risk and benefit. They distinguish between treatment-related research and nonbeneficial research, noting that treatment-related research is subject to the usual standards of professional conduct of medical practice, whereas nonbeneficial interventions—that is, those conducted for the purposes of basic research only—fall under research-related rules, including stricter requirements for obtaining consent.

U.S. Government Regulations

Since the early 1960s, the Department of Health, Education, and Welfare (DHEW) has been developing regulations for medical experimentation with humans and, more recently, for psychological experimentation and any other activity with humans that receives federal support (Curran, 1969; Gray, 1975).

Under the current DHEW system, responsibility for the protection of human subjects is shared by the Institutional Review Board at the investigator's institution, the peer review committee of nonfederal experts that evaluates the application, the staff of the funding agency, and the staff of the Office for Protection from Research Risks, DHEW. Little research was done to evaluate the adequacy of these protections until recently. One study (Barber, Lally, Makarushka, and Sullivan, 1973), for which the data were collected in 1969, showed that roughly one third of the institutional review boards surveyed had never modified a proposal for ethical reasons and that two thirds of the boards had never rejected a proposal on ethical grounds. This suggests that review by the boards at that time was probably inadequate; comparable data are not available from more recent years, although the results of a study conducted around 1976 on contract for the National Commission for the Protection of Human Subjects of Biomedical and Behavioral Research (Cooke and Tannenbaum, 1977) show that 22 percent of the boards in their sample modified one third or fewer of proposals reviewed. This suggests that board activity has increased at least somewhat since 1969, as sensitivities to ethical problems have increased. The Cooke and Tannenbaum (1977) study also confirmed the finding by Barber and others (1973) that institutional review boards' modifications of proposals are confined almost entirely to alterations in consent forms; in the 1977 study, other types of modifications were reported in fewer than 5 percent of proposals. In the recommendations section of this book, we discuss briefly some of the problems with ethics review and advisory committees.

The Professional Associations' Involvement

The American Psychological Association (APA) developed its first formal code of ethics in 1953. As recently as 1963, this was still apparently the only functioning code that had been officially adopted by a scientific organization (Cranberg, 1963), although the Nuremberg Code or variants of it have been adopted by several medical associations (Wolfensberger, 1967). The APA code has been revised several times since 1953; the latest version (American Psychological Association, 1977a) is reprinted in the back of this book. The APA has also developed more detailed statements of standards that apply to specific aspects of psychologists' activities, such as doing research (American Psychological Association, 1973), administering psychological tests (American Psychological Association, 1974), and providing psychological services (American Psychological Association, 1977b, at the end of this book).

Ethical Concerns About Behavior Modification

Increasing public concern about biomedical and behavioral research has found expression in concern about behavior modification. Some of the alarm about behavior modification arises because of the public's misunderstanding about how human behavior is modified. Other concerns stem from the public's increased appreciation of human rights in general, one aspect of which is concern about the rights of those involved in psychological interventions. Society is also becoming increasingly sensitive to the need for accountability at all levels.

Behavior modification, with its emphasis on measurement, would seem to be particularly responsive to this concern. Why, then, do so many people criticize behavior modification? What is the source of the opposition to interventions and clinical practices based on a behavioral viewpoint?

Like other psychologists, professionals using behavior modification methods evince varying levels of ethical responsibility. However, because behavioral professionals keep detailed quantitative records, their procedures and outcomes are more available for public scrutiny. Thus, the very measurements used in behavior modification and the effectiveness they demonstrate raise issues of freedom and control.

People are afraid of being controlled. The fact that some behavior analysts have claimed far-reaching abilities to control others' behavior has fed these fears, as has Skinner's (1971) much publicized critique of traditional concepts of freedom and dignity. His attack on the notion of a free and autonomous person was contrary to many people's ideals. Popular books and movies have amplified further people's fears of behavior modification, through exaggerated fictional presentations said to portray some version of behavior modification, such as *A Clockwork Orange, The Manchurian Candidate, Brave New World,* and *1984.* In the more serious press, a detailed law review critique (Heldman, 1973) argued that behavior modification could be used to "impose an orthodoxy of 'appropriate conduct' " on the community and thus to silence social and political dissent.

Some of the public concern stems from disagreement with the view of human nature that underlies the practice of behavior modification. For example, some mental health professionals have attacked behavior modification on the grounds that its underlying assumptions are at variance with their own basic values and tend to dehumanize people (Carrera and Adams, 1970). Contingency contracting has been said to foster a manipulative exchange orientation to social interaction and token economies, an emphasis on materialistic evaluation of human efforts.

Rejoinders by behavioral professionals note that behavior modification is but one example of the way in which people's behavior can be influenced and that all behavior-influencing techniques assume that people's environment has some effect on their behavior. Education, advertising, and political campaigns, for example, all attempt to alter people's behavior, and all rest on the same assumption as behavior modification, even if less formally.

Broadly speaking, influencing others is an essential aspect of social behavior. More specifically, all types of psychological interventions attempt to control people's behavior. Therapy without manipulation is a mirage that disappears on close scrutiny (Shapiro and Birk, 1967); that is, in all kinds of therapy, the therapist hopes to change the patient in some way. Bandura (1969, p. 85) has made this point especially forcefully: "In discussing moral and practical issues of behavioral control, it is essential to recognize that social influence is not a question of imposing controls where none existed before. All behavior is inevitably controlled, and the operations of psychological laws cannot be suspended by romantic conceptions of human behavior, any more than indignant rejection of the law of gravity as antihumanistic can stop people from falling. . . . The process of behavior change, therefore, involves substituting new controlling conditions for those that have regulated a person's behavior. The basic moral question is not whether man's behavior will be controlled, but rather by whom, by what means, and for what ends."

The commission's report is written from the same point of view as Bandura's statement, and the questions he raises—by whom, by what means, and for what ends—will be dealt with in subsequent sections, as well as in our recommendations.

Philosophical objections have also been expressed to behavior modification. For example, some people are concerned that, to the extent that behavior modification downplays cognition as an independent causal factor, it challenges the natural worth of human beings. Persons who make that objection hold that human rights are grounded in a degree of autonomy present in the human reason.

Also, some feel that the behaviorist view undercuts the rational justification of ethical discourse. Ethical positions can be viewed by the behaviorist as statements of the contingencies in the environment. Skinner (1971), for example, views ethical concepts as statements about the more remote consequences of our behavior, so that making a value judgment, calling something good or bad, is a way of classifying the thing in terms of its long-range reinforcing effects. In Skinner's view, positively valued things are those that are reinforcing to us, and ethical or prescriptive statements ("You should tell the truth") are indirect references to controlling contingencies ("If you tell the truth, society will generally reinforce your behavior"), including the contingencies that reinforce the behavior of the speaker ("If you tell the truth, that will reinforce my behavior"). People who object to this approach are opposed to ethics becoming a domain for causal analysis rather than for rational argument. In their opinion, the behaviorist approach to ethics removes the grounds for ethical restraint.

Other critics of behavior modification have much more specific concerns. Complaints have been voiced about the technical terms used by behavioral professionals—words like *modification, shaping,* and *control*—because of their manipulative connotations. On the other hand, the complaint has also been made that the technical language of behavior modification—words like *time out* and *aversive stimuli*—can be used euphemistically to cover up harsh procedures and to provide professional legitimation of ugly techniques.

Some critics question the empirical data base of the field and ask whether behavior modification procedures are sufficiently well demonstrated for them to be generally recommended and widely disseminated.

A common concern relates to the use of unpleasant stimuli or punishment. Some of the techniques of behavior modification involve the use of painful or unpleasant stimuli, and others require that the client be denied privileges and activities available to comparable persons in order for the behavior modification with the client to be effective.

Aversive stimuli can be used properly, with careful safeguards, including continued monitoring of the data and checks by advisory committees on the psychologists conducting the intervention. However, in some settings aversive stimuli have been misused, sometimes by persons ill-trained or untrained in behavior modification methods and sometimes by trained persons. Public alarm has risen in such cases and others when it has seemed that individuals have been treated in a way that was harsh and unwarranted.

Formal Expressions of Society's Concerns

Since the late 1960s, private organizations and foundations have been increasingly involved in programs dealing with the ethics of behavioral interventions and have called numerous conferences to explore the issues. Examples of these are the Institute of Society, Ethics, and the Life Sciences of the Hastings Center (Hastings-on-Hudson, New York), and the Behavioral Law Center of the Institute for Behavioral Research (Silver Spring, Maryland).

Since the early 1970s, court decisions having direct or indirect implications for the practice of behavior modification have been increasingly frequent. Many of these cases have involved attorneys from two organizations which were created in 1972, the Mental Health Law Project and the National Prison Project of the American Civil Liberties Union Foundation. The developing mental health case law reflects societal concern about accountability, civil liberties, and the rights of all types of disadvantaged groups, including prisoners, mental patients, and the mentally retarded.

Congressional Involvement in Behavior Modification

In addition to the activities of the courts, members of Congress have criticized behavioral technology and expressed concern about the treatment of research subjects and infringements on freedoms in therapy and research in general, as well as specifically in behavior modification. Much interest has centered on the use of behavior technology at the Medical Center for Federal Prisoners, Springfield, Missouri, in a program called the Special Treatment and Rehabilitative Training program, and given the acronym START. Hearings were held by the House of Representatives on the use of behavior modification in the START program (U.S. Congress, 1974a).

The Senate Subcommittee on Constitutional Rights, especially Senator Sam J. Ervin, Jr., also expressed concern about issues involving the constitutional rights of prisoners, in the context of a general concern for the constitutional rights of research subjects and institutionalized persons. Ervin pressed the Law Enforcement Assistance Administration (LEAA) especially concerning the behavior modification projects that it was supporting in prisons. In February 1974, the administrator of LEAA announced that he had banned the use of LEAA funds for "psychosurgery, medical research, behavior modification—including aversion therapy—and chemotherapy" (U.S. Congress, 1974b, p. 420). The use of LEAA funds for behavior modification was banned "because there are no technical and professional skills on the LEAA staff to screen, evaluate, or monitor such projects" (p. 420).

The termination of the programs was criticized by the American Psychological Association as an injustice to the public and to prison inmates. An APA news release (February 15, 1974) said that the LEAA decision would tend to "stifle the development of humane forms of treatment that provide the offender the opportunity to fully realize his or her potential as a contributing member of society." However, as events turned out, the LEAA guidelines, when they became available, were written to permit research in areas that did not involve physical or psychological risk to the prisoners, and it seems that all behavior modification programs except those using aversive control are considered not to involve such risks (U.S. Congress, 1974b).

Completing its three-year investigation of behavior modification, the Senate Subcommittee on Constitutional Rights of the Committee of the Judiciary published a report of over 600 pages on the federal role in behavior modification and the implications of behavior modification technology for individual rights (U.S. Congress, 1974b). This report documents in detail the extent of federal support for research on behavior modification, criticizes the government's involvement in such projects, and calls for "continuing legislative oversight . . . to ensure that constitutional rights and privacy are well protected" when behavior modification is used (U.S. Congress, 1974b, p. 45).

Another report generated in part by congressional concern about behavior modification programs was a paper on behavior modification from the National Institute of Mental Health (Brown, Wienckowski, and Stolz, 1975). This policy statement reviewed what is known about the efficacy of behavior modification, and dealt with some of the relevant social concerns. The report concluded (p. 24): "Professional evaluation of [behavior modification] techniques and public discussion of them can help prevent abuses in the use of behavior modification procedures, as well as foster public understanding and acceptance of beneficial procedures. . . . Both continued monitoring of behavior modifications by the public and further research on this important technology are needed to serve society and the individuals who make it up."

In 1974, Congress passed the National Research Act (PL 93–348), which, among other things, established the National Commission for the Protection of Human Subjects of Biomedical and Behavioral Research. The act also provided for the establishment of the permanent National Advisory Council for the Protection of Human Subjects within the Department of Health, Education, and Welfare. Among many other tasks, the National Commission for the Protection of Human Subjects was charged with investigating the implications for the protection of subjects of "research advances such as behavior modification."

The Professional Associations and Behavior Modification

In 1968, the American Psychiatric Association initiated the appointment of a series of task forces charged with reporting to the membership on new and controversial procedures within psychiatry. The task forces considered the available research evidence on the efficacy of the new methods, as well as their ethical implications. The fifth of these, appointed in 1971, was the Task Force on Behavior Therapy. The report of the task force concluded: "Behavior therapy and behavioral principles employed in the analysis of clinical phenomena have reached a stage of development where they now unquestionably have much to offer informed clinicians in the service of modern clinical and social psychiatry" (Birk and others, 1973, p. 64).

The Association for Advancement of Behavior Therapy (AABT) is an organization of several thousand professionals, including psychologists, psychiatrists, and social workers, who are interested in behavior therapy and behavior modification. The AABT in 1974 developed a system of consultative committees coordinated by the president of the association. Persons who are concerned about present or proposed behavior therapy programs or procedures, especially in institutions, can ask the AABT president to appoint a committee to go to the site, investigate, and make an advisory report. Several such site visits are conducted each year.

A Brief Overview of the Commission's Report

The next section of this book discusses the major ethical issues that arise whenever behavior modification and other psychological interventions are used. In the commission's analysis of these issues, we stress protections for the rights of the recipient of the intervention. The commission members discussed at length the relative weight that should be given to individual rights and society's rights. A balance has to be achieved, of course. On the basis of our discussions and the materials that we read, we chose to emphasize the client's rights, and that is the point of view throughout the rest of the report.

Subsequent chapters take up special problems that arise when interventions occur in out-patient settings, institutions for the mentally ill and mentally retarded, schools, and prisons. Behavior

TWO

Ethics of Interventions: The Major Issues

In its analysis of the intervention process, the APA Commission on Behavior Modification identified issues that are important in considering psychological interventions:

- Identification of the client
- Definition of the problem and selection of goals
- Selection of the intervention method
- Accountability
- Evaluation of the quality of the psychologist and the intervention
- Record keeping and confidentiality
- Protection of the client's rights
- Assessment of the place of research in therapeutic settings

Each of these issues arises whenever psychological interventions are used, although some of them are more salient in some settings than in others. Ethical dilemmas—for behavior modification and all other kinds of psychological intervention—arise when the professional and the individual whose behavior is to be changed are from different social classes or have different statuses (and hence have different values or differential access to reinforcers), when the voluntary nature of the involvement of the persons whose behavior is to be changed is compromised in any way, when their competence to enter into an agreement regarding the intervention is questionable, or when people are subjected to interventions they do not realize are in effect.

This chapter will discuss those aspects of the issues that apply across most or all settings; to the extent that any issue has special pertinence for a particular setting, it will be discussed in the chapter that follows on ethical issues raised in case studies of that setting. In addition, our recommendations also pertain to these key issues.

Identification of the Client

Discussion of psychological interventions entails mention of the psychologist's client. However, who or what the "client" is may not be obvious. In our view, the term *client* has two meanings, and discussions of the ethics of psychological interventions become ambiguous when distinctions are not made between these two meanings.

In one sense, the client may be the person whose behavior is to be changed, the person who is the target of the intervention. In another sense, the client may be the person, institution, agency, or community who is paying the psychologist; that is, the psychologist's employer. In out-patient settings, these two roles are usually filled by the same individual. Often, however, they are not, and when the person paying the psychologist is not the one whose behavior is to be changed, ethical issues usually arise. In our discussions in this book, we will separate these two roles whenever such a distinction is required.

Ethics of Interventions: The Major Issues

In the practice of behavior modification, the person whose behavior is to be changed is often different from the person or institution paying the psychologist. Further, those whose behavior is to be changed through a behavioral intervention are often from a lower socioeconomic stratum or of lower status than the psychologist, and the psychologist's wages and employment tend to be controlled by the administrators of an institution, corporation, agency, or some other group of people.

All these relationships are important in an analysis of the ethical protections of an intervention, because they all relate to the extent to which different people involved in the intervention can exercise control and countercontrol. Control of another person's behavior is possible when one has access to whatever reinforces that person. Countercontrol is the reciprocal of control: It is the influence the controllee has on the controller by virtue of access to suitable reinforcers. In an out-patient setting, only the professional and the client are involved, and each may attempt to influence the other. When significant reinforcers are held by the agency employing the professional, however, the professional's behavior is subject to control by both the employing agency and the client. Only when the client also has access to reinforcers for the professional's behavior can the client's countercontrol be effective.

A Note on Countercontrol

A distinction can be made between an applied behavior analysis approach to countercontrol and a social learning conceptualization of it. Although a detailed consideration of such differences is beyond the scope of this report, we will briefly present the way that each of these models describes this phenomenon.

Countercontrol, in the context of applied behavior analysis, is defined as already discussed—the control the person whose behavior is to be changed exercises over the behavior of the person attempting to induce behavior change. As noted, countercontrol in this sense requires that the client have access to relevant contingencies for the psychologist's behavior. Possible reinforcers would include the fee for service and data demonstrating that the client's behavior is or is not changing.

The term *countercontrol,* in the context of social learning theory, refers to an individual's ability to resist external influence in spite of prevailing environmental contingencies (Davison, 1973). Bandura (1974) has objected to the use of the term *countercontrol* on the grounds that it misleadingly portrays the individual as a mere reactor to environmental instigation, rather than as an active initiator of behavioral and environmental change. In the terms of social learning theory, this portrayal implies that the involved participation of the person whose behavior is being modified is usually imperative if durable behavior change is to result (see, for example, Mahoney, 1974; Wilson and Evans, in press).

In many respects, however, the applied behavior analysis approach and the social learning theory conceptualization are simply two different ways of stating the same relationships. Applied behavior analysis, for example, would contend that "involved participation" could be operationally defined as the psychologist's having reinforcers for the client's behavior; without these, durable behavior change will not occur. Also, people's "ability to resist external influences" would be said to be behaviors that are a function of their history of reinforcement for that particular class of behavior.

Implications of the Two Meanings of Client

The definition of the term *client* is critical in the analysis of the ethics of interventions, because the clients should actively participate in establishing the goals and means of treatment, and the therapist should be accountable to them. Many of the other issues raised in this report also have to do with the relationship of the professional and the client.

Because the term *client* has two meanings, we have made clear, whenever the word is used in this book, which meaning we are using—the person whose behavior is to be changed or the person employing the psychologist. Many protective mechanisms, such as informed consent, in psychological interventions will take quite different forms depending on which "client" is consulted. Most especially, because the persons employing the psychologists will usually have access to more powerful reinforcers than will the persons whose behavior is to be changed, psychologists may often find it difficult to oppose their employers' wishes for the clients. For this reason, some professionals question whether psychological interventions should ever be used when the people being modified are not the psychologists' employers. In its most radical form, this position would prevent the use of psychological interventions not only with prisoners but also with children, retarded persons, the senile aged, and psychotics. Denying treatment to such persons is abhorrent, in our opinion, and special procedures will be discussed later that attempt to protect the rights of persons who cannot employ psychologists and yet who would benefit from psychological interventions. Furthermore, the issue of the definition of the term *client* will be dealt with extensively later in this book, along with other issues.

Definition of the Problem and Selection of Goals

Whenever an intervention is contemplated, a decision must be made about whether there is a problem, what that problem is, and what the desired outcome of the intervention would be. Some behaviors are defined as inappropriate by virtually all members of society; other behaviors are widely valued. An intervention program designed to eliminate the former class of behaviors and increase the latter would raise few complaints about its goals. The ethical dilemmas arise when people disagree about whether a given behavior is a problem and whether some other behavior is a suitable goal. Such disagreements can concern the short-term value of these behaviors as well as their value for society in the long run.

Decisions about the definition of the problem and the selection of goals will involve both the professional's and the client's values. One view of values is that they refer to the long-range reinforcers associated with a given behavior (Skinner, 1971); in this view, identifying the cultural norm by labeling a behavior as good or ethical is an additional, more immediate consequence that functions to maintain the behavior. Thus, as in the preceding section on the identification of the client, the issue centers on the access to reinforcers. Defining the problem and selecting the goals of the intervention are both classes of behavior under the control of the immediate reinforcers in the setting and of those long-range reinforcers or values that also control the professional's and the client's behavior.

Ideally, the goals of interventions would be selected so as to be congruent with the long-term good of society as a whole. Unfortunately, in practice there is no way to determine either what the long-term good of society is or what impact any immediate decision will have in the long run.

In all settings, ethical protections will be enhanced if all those involved specify, to the extent possible, those reinforcers that may be functioning to control their own behavior. The professional and the professional's employer might, for example, specify their systems of values and attitudes relating to the client's problem.

Selection of the Intervention Method

Issues involved in the selection of the method of intervention are closely related to those involved in the selection of goals. Here, too, the decision or selection is behavior that is under the control of reinforcers. Possible reinforcers for the selection of specific interventions include information about the efficacy and risks of various methods, feedback from the professional's supervisors and peers, and the professional's and client's values. All these factors are influential in the selection of an intervention method, although some of them may be more potent than others in some settings and under some circumstances.

Currently, court decisions have stressed the use of the least intrusive and restrictive intervention, the most benign, practical, and economical in implementation (Wexler, 1973). One analysis (Maley and Hayes, 1975) has suggested that in practice the least restrictive alternative is simply that with the least obvious control.

More intrusive and restrictive interventions are those where the control tends to be through punishment, threat of punishment, deprivation of positive reinforcement, or the use of positive reinforcement in a barren environment or where the reinforcers are so strong that compliance is very likely. Maley and Hayes' argument is that our language restricts the use of such terms as *intrusive* and *restrictive* to those interventions where the controlling events are more obvious and punitive. Even though behavioral principles imply that positive controls are also coercive, the legal and commonsense uses of the term *coercion* are limited to controls perceived as aversive.

Because of court rulings regarding the "least restrictive alternative," some guidelines that have been proposed recommend a hierarchical procedure in which less restrictive procedures are attempted and must be shown to be ineffective prior to the introduction of more intrusive and restrictive techniques (for example, see May, Risley, Twardosz, Friedman, Bijou, Wexler, and others, 1975). May and others (1975) advocate recourse to procedures designed to weaken behavior only in those cases where reinforcement of positive alternative behaviors has failed to overcome a problem that interferes with the client's progress. Again, with procedures aimed at weakening behavior, as with those used to strengthen behavior, these guidelines recommend a hierarchy of interventions (for example, soft reprimands would be used before overcorrection, which in turn might precede seclusion or time out).

What little empirical evidence there is on this point suggests that sequencing intervention strategies from least to more restrictive—that is, from least to more obvious control—may, under some circumstances, undermine the efficacy of a program. For example, O'Leary, Becker, Evans, and Saudargas (1969) introduced rules, structure, and a combination of praising and ignoring as treatment components prior to instituting a token economy. Disruptive behavior was reduced only during the token economy. The question is whether an earlier introduction of the token program might not have produced behavior change more efficiently and effectively. Although controlled comparisons were not made, O'Leary anecdotally reports his impression that the token economy that was eventually introduced in the O'Leary and others (1969) study resulted in less behavior change than previous studies with similar populations in which token programs were introduced earlier in the treatment. Thus, inflexibly sequencing intervention strategies from the least severe to the most severe might well have adverse effects, in the sense that a program so sequenced might be less effective than one that began with a stronger intervention.

Whether professionals begin with the least severe of all possible interventions will depend only partially on the data available regarding the comparative efficacy of such sequencing. Other factors influencing professionals' decisions on how to proceed will be their values and the short- and long-term contingencies on their behavior, including potential feedback from their peers and the clients' community.

Aversive Techniques

Some of the methods used in behavior therapy rely for their effectiveness on their ability to decelerate behavior. These include the methods of aversion therapy, which are based primarily on a classical conditioning paradigm, and operant punishment techniques, which may be either the addition of an aversive stimulus or the removal of a positive reinforcer after inappropriate behavior. Most people think of the addition of an aversive stimulus when "aversive control" is mentioned.

Although many therapeutic approaches use some form of aversive control, behavior modification appears to be unique in clearly identifying and labeling these methods as aversive. As a consequence, criticism directed at behavior modification methods seems equally applicable to other uses of aversive control, such as criticism of the client by the psychologist, physical attacks, open confrontation between the client and the psychologist or other clients, and other such techniques used in contemporary psychotherapies (for example, see Corsini, 1973). Furthermore, whether a technique is labeled aversive or positive depends often simply on one's choice of words. Escape or avoidance contingencies can be translated into positive reinforcement contingencies by a semantic shift. For example, stimuli that signal escape from hunger or thirst can also be considered to signal the acquisition of food or water; stimuli associated with escape from or avoidance of abandonment, neglect, or shame, may also be said to signal love and approval.

As with other intervention techniques, whether aversive methods are used will depend on the psychologist's assessment of the available data on the efficacy of those techniques with the particular population and behavior problem involved, on the reactions of the psychologist's peers and the client's community to the use of those techniques, and on the psychologist's own values. The process of selection of aversive treatments, like that for all other treatments, should involve a specification of those influential factors.

The commission might have taken an explicit stand in opposition to the use of aversive stimuli in therapy. We did not, partly because of the semantic problem already noted of identifying which techniques are aversive; partly because aversive techniques are widely used, are effective, and are accepted in contemporary psychotherapy (Corsini, 1973); and partly because these techniques are sometimes either the only effective ones or else the only ones effective within the limits of other considerations. In the treatment of self-injurious behavior in autistic children, for example, punishment produces extremely rapid cessation of this destructive response, whereas the positive techniques currently known take considerably longer and hence expose the child to a much longer period of self-injury. Psychologists whose values include minimizing the client's pain and disfigurement, as well as limitations on the client's mobility from restraints, are likely to select a punishment therapy, at least until more rapidly effective positive treatments are devised.

Accountability

Measurement of the behaviors under study is a virtually universal characteristic of behavior modification practice. Because "side effects"—changes in behaviors that are not the target of intervention—are possible in behavior modification, just as in other psychological interventions, a number of behaviors in addition to those targeted for change should be monitored. The published literature in behavior modification suggests that when behavioral procedures are used, both positive and negative changes may occur in the client's other behaviors.

Information about the direct and indirect results of an intervention enables those who are concerned about the results—such as the person whose behavior is being modified, the person who is paying the professional, and the representatives of any agency or institution involved—to get feedback on its progress. Further, continuing collection of data enables modification of the intervention as necessary, in response to the progress or lack of progress in the client's behavior.

In all settings, regular and reliable data collection and analysis are prerequisites for quality assurance. Those responsible for interventions must recognize the time and effort that data collection and analysis entail, so that appropriate resources are allocated.

Wolf (in press) has suggested that professionals obtain social validation of the results of an intervention by asking those whose behavior was changed and others in their environment for such an evaluation. Although, on the one hand, consumer satisfaction would seem an important concomitant of a successful program, on the other hand, some professionals would argue that ensuring "maximum conformity with contemporary cultural values" (Roos, 1974, p. 6), which the social validation procedure would seem to do, might not necessarily be an optimum goal. Behavioral interventions, like other psychological interventions, can act to strengthen existing societal practices or can help to engineer social change. To the extent that the persons to whom the program is accountable have influence on the design of the program, the decision about who those persons will be will influence the social impact of the program. For example, in a program conducted in the public schools, it is possible that the evaluation the children would make of the social validity of an intervention might be quite different from the evaluation made by their parents and teachers; the latter evaluation might be different again from an evaluation made by peers of the professional conducting the program.

Evaluation of the Quality of the Psychologist and the Intervention

The specific personal and professional qualifications necessary for a competent behavioral psychologist have not been determined. Martin (1974) and Risley (1975), for example, conclude that procedures should be certified, rather than persons. Procedures may be certified, but this solution is partial at best, because the appropriateness and effectiveness of a given procedure is always relative to the particular population of clients, the particular setting, and the particular professional delivering the procedure. Consequently, the thorny problem of certification of behavioral professionals remains. Agras (1973, p. 169) summed up contemporary clinical (behavioral) lore when he noted that the behavior therapist "must have knowledge of the principles underlying behavior modification, experience in the application of such knowledge to human behavior problems, and experience in the experimental analysis of deviant human behavior, both for research purposes and as an approach to the ongoing evaluation of clinical care. He must also, however, demonstrate certain less well-defined characteristics, usually referred to as general clinical skills." The latter skills may be acquired in graduate training programs in clinical or school psychology, with required internship experiences, or they may be learned on the job in supervised practice.

Sulzer-Azaroff, Thaw, and Thomas (1975) surveyed persons active in the evaluation of research in behavior modification, asking them to rate various behaviors in regard to what they felt was essential for a competent behavioral professional. The researchers found no clear support for a system to determine the competency of an individual to perform behavior modification, and they suggested that where and by whom an individual is trained might serve as the prime guides for competence in behavior modification, so long as direct, objective evidence is lacking. However, they advocate that competence be evaluated in reference to criterion behaviors.

The training and competence of paraprofessionals or mediators of behavior change programs also demand careful consideration. Behavioral psychologists in charge of an intervention program must ensure the adequacy of training of their staff and continued supervision of ongoing programs. Effective pre- and in-service teacher training programs have been described (for example, see Rollins, McCandless, Thompson, and Brassell, 1974). Specific behavioral training methods like modeling and behavior rehearsal are important in addition to didactic instruction, as are observations made in the target environment subsequent to the training.

Evaluation of the adequacy of an intervention is a continual process beginning with the initiation of the intervention and continuing through the followup. If the initial intervention does not achieve its goals, the professional and client reconsider their decisions about the treatment and discuss the possibility of trying alternative interventions.

Whatever the consequences of the initial intervention, evaluation includes continual monitoring throughout the duration of the intervention, as well as the generalization of behavior change to other settings and the maintenance of improvement over time. Because these different processes might be governed by different variables, explicit strategies should be considered for producing generalization and maintenance once the initial effects have been demonstrated. Approaches to producing generalization can emphasize programming the environment or programming the individual's behavior (Stokes and Baer, 1977). These different strategies are not, of course, mutually exclusive.

Record Keeping and Confidentiality

The major issues related to record keeping and confidentiality are how the confidentiality of the records on the intervention is maintained, who has access to those records, and who controls access to the records. If videotaping is used for educational or training purposes, issues of the client's consent are relevant. Recent legal rulings have given clients and their guardians access to the clients' own files and the opportunity to discuss any erroneous information in them. In our view, the issues of record keeping and confidentiality are general to all psychological interventions; behavior modification appears to raise no unique problems in this respect.

Protection of the Client's Rights

Mechanisms designed to protect the client's rights in psychological interventions vary greatly from setting to setting, so that most of the relevant issues will be taken up in each of the subsequent chapters devoted to specific settings. For many settings, however, the recommendation is made that an advisory committee be constituted to help develop and supervise the intervention and to review procedures to ensure that they are ethical. The membership of such committees is generally supposed to include representatives of those whose behavior is to be modified, their guardians or advocates, former clients, clients' family members, peers of the professional, clergy, attorneys, and sometimes members of such social groups as the poor or minorities.

Establishing such a committee does not ensure an ethical intervention, however. The behavior of the members of the advisory committee, like all other behavior, will be under the control of reinforcers. The official guardians of the participants in an intervention may have a vested interest in controlling them in a way more convenient (and reinforcing) for the guardians than beneficial for their wards (Friedman, 1975). If outside members of the advisory committee are paid by the client institution, they will be subject to its control to some extent, and the more important the money is to them, the more they will be controlled.

Such an advisory committee does, however, provide a regularized opportunity for conflicting points of view to be expressed, and the group's discussions may sensitize program administrators to the conflicting interests involved. The advisory committee will influence programs only to the extent that it has access to reinforcers. The procedures establishing the committee can be designed to maximize the committee's power by requiring its approval prior to the initiation of any program, for example, or by giving the committee the power to control the behavior of staff through fines, bonuses, or other comparable measures (Burton, 1974).

It is obviously not feasible for advisory committees associated with large institutions or with community mental health centers with large catchment areas to review and approve treatment programs for all clients in advance, but they might review a sample of procedures retrospectively.

Informed Consent

The legal use of the term *informed consent* refers to the clients' right to decide whether they want to participate in a proposed program, after they have been told what is going to be involved. More specifically, informed consent is considered to have three components: knowledge, voluntariness, and competency (Friedman, 1975). The term *knowledge* refers to the information describing the program and its goals, explaining that individuals may refuse to participate in the program before it begins or at any time during the program, and offering alternative programs. The term *voluntariness* refers to the absence of coercion or duress when the decision to consent is made. The term *competency* reflects an assessment that the clients can understand the information that has been given to them and make a judgment about it (Friedman, 1975; Martin, 1975).

Whether clients have been given the information necessary to meet the "knowledge" requirement can be assessed objectively by testing them on the material. Similarly, their competence to make the necessary decisions is, at least in principle, subject to objective assessment. The part of informed consent most difficult to deal with in the context of behavior modification is the component of voluntariness. Goldiamond (1969) suggests that behavior can be called voluntary when a range of alternative responses is available, with a range of positive consequences contingent on them (see also Krasner, 1965). Also, behavior is often described as voluntary when aversive or coercive control is absent (Maley and Hayes, 1975).

Because of the difficulties of fitting the notion of informed consent into a behavioral framework, several authors have suggested alternative methods for dealing with this concept, methods more consistent with a behavioral approach. Davison and Stuart (1975), for example, have proposed a hierarchy of constraints on the giving of consent; Goldiamond (1974) has described a schema relating consent to the extent to which the contingencies in the environment are coercive. Schwitzgebel (1975) conceptualizes treatment as a contractual activity, in which the outcomes are specified in advance, with explicit contingencies for success or failure. In that context, he recommends contracts instead of consent as a way to protect or at least clarify clients' rights. Contract law, he says, already prohibits fraud, misrepresentation, and duress in the treatment situation.

The populations that tend to be involved in behavior modification programs are those for whom some aspect of informed consent may be questionable; the relevant issues will be taken up in the sections of the report that follow.

Assessment of the Place of Research in Therapeutic Settings

In many ways, the goals and methods of research are not identical with those of clinical evaluation. This section is concerned with the use of research methodologies for the evaluation of the efficacy of established (or relatively established) therapeutic methods.

A common method for evaluating the efficacy of behavior modification has been the "reversal" procedure. In applying this procedure, a successful intervention is deliberately stopped to see if the client then gets worse. If the newly acquired behavior deteriorates when the intervention is stopped and then recovers when it is reintroduced, this is strong evidence that the behavior change was a consequence of the intervention. This methodology, unfortunately, requires the client to get worse in order to demonstrate the efficacy of the program. Extended reversals are thus indefensible; briefer ones are often not acceptable to the clients and others involved.

One alternative to extended reversals is the use of brief probes (Bijou, Peterson, Harris, Allen, and Johnston, 1969) in which the intervention is stopped for only a short period of time. In one sense, a probe that is initiated to see whether the behavior will worsen when the intervention is terminated, in order to demonstrate the control of the procedures of the program, is simply a minireversal, and the clients are likely to have the same objections to this procedure as to more extended reversals (Stolz, 1976). On the other hand, the goal of all interventions is to have the client maintain improvement after the intervention has been terminated. A brief interruption in the program can be used to test whether the client's behavior has become independent of the contingencies and responsive to natural consequences. The expectation in this case would be that the client's behavior would not worsen during the probe period. If it did, the program would be resumed, and further attempts would be made to extend the control of natural contingencies. Probes can also be used to demonstrate to persons in the client's environment that the client's behavior is responsive to their behavior.

An alternative design coming into increasing use is the multiple-baseline control procedure (Baer, Wolf, and Risley, 1968). In this procedure, several different behaviors are monitored at once, but consequences are introduced initially only for one of the behaviors, later for a second, and still later for others. If only those behaviors improve that have been subjected to the intervention, the professional can conclude that the intervention was responsible for the changes observed. Alternatively, the intervention can be made across a number of behaviors but in only one of several settings, while the behavior is monitored in all of the settings. Consequences are later introduced in the remaining settings, one at a time. Again, if the behavior changes only in the settings in which the intervention has been introduced, the professional can conclude that the intervention was responsible for the changes observed.

An issue that arises with respect to this procedure is that the psychologist is temporarily denying treatment for some aspects of the client's behavior, because only one behavior at a time is subjected to the intervention, or else the client is being treated in only one setting at a time. If the intervention is generally acknowledged to be effective, denying it simply to achieve a multiple-baseline design might be unethical. Another problem with the multiple-baseline design is that if the behavioral intervention produces widespread change in the client's behavior, change will occur in behaviors or settings not currently subject to the intervention. In that case, the multiple-baseline design will be a "failure" as a research design, even though the intervention would have been a success.

However, in practice it may be hard for clients to learn to administer consequences to a number of different behaviors simultaneously so that something like a multiple-baseline design may be necessary to teach them to use behavioral techniques. Furthermore, as a pragmatic matter, before extending a procedure to more aspects of a client's life, an intervention should probably be tried out on one or a few behaviors, to ensure that the intervention works with the client.

An alternative to individual subject designs is group comparison designs. Many of these involve a control group that receives no intervention. That is, when such a group is used, certain clients are told that they will not receive any special training. Permission is necessary so that the clients can be evaluated and their records made available. However, many people object to the use of a nontreated group on the grounds that control-group clients would feel deprived and charge that necessary services were being denied.

As an alternative to having a group of clients receive no treatment or simply receive attention but not an effective treatment, Stuart (1973) proposes the use of contrast groups (groups that receive a different form of treatment) and group-monitoring procedures. In the latter, a no-treatment control group would be used, but clients' progress would be deliberately monitored in order to detect any worsening of their behavior. Clients showing deterioration would then be assigned to active treatment. The use of group monitoring with possible assignment to active treatment undermines the design, however, because methodologically lethal, differential

THREE

Out-Patient Settings

This chapter considers ethical issues highlighted by the use of behavior modification in out-patient settings, including private offices, clinics, out-patient departments, and the out-patient services of community mental health centers. Community mental health agencies differ in one important respect from the other settings discussed in this chapter, in that they are more directly financed by the community. The other settings are linked to parts of the community more or less loosely (as when payment is by third parties) or not at all (as when the client pays all of the fee). This last is a diminishing portion of the client population.

Clients treated in these settings include adults, adolescents, and children labeled as nonhospitalized psychotics, neurotics, and nonsociopathic personality disorders, as well as adults reporting marital and other situational problems. These out-patient facilities also often treat persons whose behavior threatens others or harms property and those who transgress social norms, such as child-abusing parents, alcoholics, addicts, and people whose sexual behavior is unconventional.

Out-patient settings present special problems with respect to the issues of identification of the client, definition of the problem and selection of goals, and accountability. Although behavior analysis, by virtue of its mode of procedure, brings these issues more sharply into focus, the issues apply in much the same way to all forms of psychological intervention. Moreover, the other major issues considered in this report, such as record keeping, confidentiality, and protection of the client's rights, apply also in out-patient settings. They are not discussed specifically in this chapter because no special additional considerations are involved over and above those discussed in Chapter Two.

Identification of the Client

The issue of identifying who the client is would seem to be least troublesome in out-patient settings, where middle-class adults define themselves as in need of treatment and pay the psychologist's fee. Even in this seemingly simple example, however, there are ethical concerns.

Although it is sometimes true that the people who present themselves at the psychologist's door are the appropriate target of the psychologist's efforts, it is not always so. If clients are living with their family, the problem often stems at least partly from the interaction among the family members. Thus, although at first the individual who hired the psychologist may have seemed to be the only client involved, further analysis of the family situation may suggest that the family as a whole should participate in the intervention. In that case, the other family members become clients as well and should be given the same consideration as the individual originally requesting assistance. Like that individual, they have, for example, the right to refuse to participate in an intervention.

Some out-patient clients lack the access to reinforcers for the psychologist that a middle-class adult would have. For example, some clients enter therapy under some degree of coercion; such clients include persons whose behavior has harmed others, damaged property, or violated laws and also include alcoholics and addicts. Frequently, for example, such clients are ordered to participate in treatment as a condition of parole, the alternative being incarceration. Youths and children may be told to get treatment to avoid being expelled from school. The psychologist's client in such cases is not only the individual undertaking treatment but also society or the agency of society that has sent the client to treatment. In such instances, where the psychologist has dual allegiance, special efforts need to be made to ensure that the client is aware of the influences on the psychologist's behavior. Furthermore, the psychologist may want to consider refusing to accept such referrals, rather than becoming society's agent, should society's goals for the client be at variance with the psychologist's values.

When children and adolescents are the psychologist's clients, the question of dual allegiance again arises; here the psychologist has allegiance both to the young persons and to their parents. Full specification of the relevant reinforcers for each of the parties, in this and the preceding cases, will maximize the opportunity for those with little power to exercise countercontrol.

Definition of the Problem and Selection of Goals

The preceding chapter noted the major role in the definition of the problem and the selection of the goals of treatment that is played by the individuals who have access to the immediate reinforcers in the setting. In the out-patient setting, the clients have the greatest access to immediate reinforcers for the psychologist, specifically the fees and their cooperation with the intervention. Because of clients' access to this potentially powerful countercontrol, the psychologist may have a problem in becoming established as the source of reinforcement for the clients and hence as a source of influence over their behavior.

Aiding the psychologist is the fact that, simply because the clients have come for assistance, they are predisposed to accept the psychologist's guidance. When clients know in advance who will be their psychologist, which is the situation prevailing in private practice, they are especially likely to value any suggestions made, and the psychologist is not likely to have a problem in becoming a source of reinforcement for the client's behavior. In contrast, when clients are assigned to psychologists in an out-patient service, the psychologists may have to use special procedures to establish their credibility. However, here they are aided by the fact that they may be considered competent simply because they are members of the clinic's staff. The clinic's reputation affects the way the psychologists are perceived.

No matter how objective and impartial they try to be, psychologists often convey their own preferences to their clients. The ethical issue, then, does not hinge on whether psychologists influence their clients' decisions—they cannot avoid doing so—but on the extent to which the psychologists specify those reinforcers that may be functioning to control their own behavior, that is, the psychologists' own value systems. Thus an important part of psychologists' ethical responsibility is monitoring their own behavior.

In short, clients' apparent freedom of choice in out-patient settings should not delude psychologists into minimizing their own responsibility for the clients' welfare. Therapists inevitably influence clients' decisions, even when ostensibly leaving them free to choose. Ethical responsibility, therefore, requires that psychologists inform the clients of their own motives and biases and, likewise, that they assist the clients in specifying those factors controlling their be-behavior. The selection of the goals of the intervention should be made in the context of as full a specification as possible of the consequences of this decision for the clients' lives and the lives of others.

Accountability

Psychologists working in community mental health centers, financed by community agencies, are accountable to their governing boards. The ethical issues associated with divided responsibility, discussed earlier in this section, apply here as well.

Out-Patient Settings

A special problem of accountability in out-patient settings arises because the interactions between the psychologist and the client are frequently on a one-to-one basis, with no other professional being necessarily responsible for the client. Thus, the psychologist and the client must be especially alert to identify subtle coercions, because the only other protection built into the system is the client's option to terminate the relationship.

To what extent does the staff of a community mental health agency have a responsibility to try to produce changes in the life of the community as a whole? Community psychology focuses on factors in the community, rather than on individual therapy; other psychologists feel that intervening in the community can create divisiveness within both the community and the agency. When psychologists employed by a community are planning intervention at the community level, the ethical issues discussed in this book—who the client is, how the goals are selected, and so on—need to be considered at that level and need to be discussed with the community agency to which the psychologists are accountable.

Summary and Conclusions

In the out-patient setting, clients typically have greater access to reinforcers for the psychologist's behavior than they do in the institutional settings discussed subsequently in this book. Even so, the psychologist can exercise considerable control over clients' behavior. We suggest that ethical practice requires that the relevant contingencies on the psychologist's and clients' behavior be explicitly stated by the psychologist as an integral part of the therapy.

FOUR

Institutions

The staff of institutions for the mentally ill, mentally retarded, and senile older persons have long complained of the difficulty of involving such residents in therapeutic programs. After publicity began to come out regarding the success of Ayllon and Azrin's (1965, 1968) pioneering use of token economies to motivate institutional residents, the procedure was adopted quickly and widely. Token economies promised to involve residents in programs in a way that staff had hoped for and typically been unable to achieve.

No epidemiological data exist to demonstrate the extent to which token economies and other behavior modification technology are currently used in institutions for the mentally ill, mentally retarded, and senile older persons, but anecdotal reports suggest that thousands of such programs are probably in effect throughout the country. This chapter discusses the issues raised by the use of behavior modification in such institutions.

Ethical Issues in Behavior Modification

Identification of the Client

Identification of the client is a particularly knotty problem in institutions for the mentally ill, mentally retarded, and aged, because of the legally determined incompetence of most such residents.

In some of the situations we examined, the psychologists' client was not the resident; rather, it was, variously, the institution's staff, a guardian, the community, or even the governor of the state. In these situations, interventions often include goals and procedures that are more in the interest of the agency than the resident. Treatment programs that are controlled by others but seemingly in the interests of the resident are usually described as "paternalistic."

Because the psychologist is so likely to have dual allegiance when working in an institution, special attention needs to be paid to protection of the clients' rights. The mechanisms that might be used are discussed later under that heading.

Definition of the Problem and Selection of Goals

A major problem in institutions for the mentally ill is that of setting goals. This problem is even more severe in institutions for the mentally retarded and aged. In these institutions, the residents tend to be passive and may not be competent to participate in the process of setting goals. At one state institution for the mentally ill that the commission visited, we were told it was very difficult to involve the chronic residents in goal selection because they do not recognize that their behavior is a problem in many cases, and often they seem not to want to change or leave the hospital.

When clients do not participate directly in goal selection, the danger is great that the institution staff will tend to select goals according to their own self-interest. The major goal often becomes making the residents less disruptive and more cooperative. Although teaching basic self-care skills, such as toothbrushing or toileting, to mentally retarded individuals is likely to be noncontroversial, other program goals, such as the reduction or elimination of aggressive behavior, are more controversial. For these, special mechanisms to protect the residents' rights need to be developed; these are discussed in a later part of this section.

Selection of the Intervention Method

Selection of the intervention method may raise special problems in residential facilities for the mentally ill, retarded, and aged, for the same reasons as goal selection. Institution staff will select treatments in response to environmental contingencies on their own behavior, as well as their own values. Because the staff in many residential facilities are underpaid and overworked, they will tend to select the treatment that is easiest to deliver, rather than taking the additional time and trouble needed to select the optimum form of therapy for each individual client. Thus treatment selection poses special problems when residents are incompetent to decide for themselves about what method should be used.

To ensure meaningful implementation of residents' right to treatment or habilitation, a range of therapeutic approaches should be available. Here again, protection of residents' rights requires special mechanisms.

Protection of the Client's Rights

Even though institutionalized persons may have more limitations on their behavioral repertoire than do the noninstitutionalized, they often are able to participate in decisions related to an intervention; when this is so, institutionalized persons then are able to act to protect their own rights. More typically, however, residents are not able to make the necessary responses, and others may act in their stead to protect the residents' rights.

Informed Consent

The three elements of informed consent are knowledge, voluntariness, and competency. With the institutionalized retarded, mentally ill, and aged, competency becomes one of the main issues.

Many persons in mental institutions and a small but still significant number of persons in institutions for the aged and the mentally retarded will be competent to make decisions about treatment goals and means. The issue of competence is a complicated one, however. Defining competency to consent is a difficult undertaking, particularly because competency may be situation specific. No universally accepted standard or procedure exists for the measurement of competence.

The goals in selecting a standard of competence are, on the one hand, to enhance self-autonomy and guard against paternalism and, on the other, to provide for vicarious judgment for residents when necessary. One view has it that competency to consent should be defined as the ability of a client to understand and act knowingly on the information provided. In practice, paper-and-pencil assessment measures are currently used to evaluate residents' competence. Behavioral psychologists seem ideally qualified to develop tasks that could be used to provide an objective, behavioral assessment of residents' understanding of information given them and their ability to act knowingly on that information.

Where residents are judged to be competent, their consent must also be voluntary and informed. Securing voluntary consent from persons in institutions for the mentally ill, mentally retarded, or aged, is of course, a difficult problem. One court observed that "involuntarily confined mental patients live in an inherently coercive institutional environment. Indirect and subtle psychological coercion has a profound effect upon the patient population."* Although that court went on to conclude that involuntarily confined mental patients could not, by virtue of their confinement and low status, give informed consent, the ruling dealt primarily with consent to psychosurgery. It seems unlikely that it will be extended to prohibit competent mental patients and other institutionalized residents from giving their consent to participate in psychological programs (Budd and Baer, 1976).

* *Kaimowitz* v. *Department of Mental Health for the State of Michigan,* Mental Disability Law Reporter 147, 151 (1976) (Mich. Cir. Ct., Wayne County, July 10, 1973).

It is true, however, that institutionalized residents are dependent on the goodwill of the staff for release from the institution and also are subject to more subtle forms of coercion related to the privileges that an involuntarily detained resident may be allowed to exercise within the institution, such as having a lamp in one's room or being allowed to use the canteen. This is not to say that consent is impossible in an institutional setting, but rather that consent must be carefully scrutinized if residents are asked to waive constitutionally protected rights or to undergo hazardous or intrusive procedures.

When residents have been objectively demonstrated to lack the competence to decide about participation in treatment or to cooperate in determining the goals of treatment, consent may be given by a parent or guardian, and the proposed procedures and the adequacy of the consent may be evaluated by an advisory panel.

Other Protective Mechanisms

When residents do not play an active role in goal selection, some other person or group, like an advisory panel, will have to decide about goals. As noted in the chapter on general issues, the people in such a group will have their own interests in relation to the choice of goals, and these should be specified as part of the goal selection process. Other aspects of the use of an advisory panel are also discussed in that chapter.

If the residents who are to participate in an intervention are judged to be incompetent, one or more persons may be appointed to represent them as a patient advocate. Unfortunately, simply appointing such individuals does not ensure that the residents' interests will be fully protected. Ideally, patient advocates should regard the resident as their primary client (Friedman, 1975). If advocates are to be effective in protecting the clients, they should have appropriate in-service training to familiarize them with relevant state and constitutional law concerning their clients' rights, as well as with techniques for effectively representing their clients. The advocates need to be independent of the power structure of the institution and to have access to reinforcers for the administrators and staff of the institution as well. Only in that way can they exercise effective countercontrol.

If members of the staff of the institution take the role of patient advocates, they are likely to be ineffective because of conflicts of interest. At one of the institutions we examined, patient advocates were staff members of the institution; although they could conduct investigations into allegations of patient abuse, they could only make recommendations to the superintendent of the institution, and they said he often declined to follow their recommendations.

Summary and Conclusions

Conducting any form of treatment in institutions for the mentally ill, mentally retarded, and senile elderly poses thorny ethical problems because the residents are often unable or unwilling to participate in the decisions made prior to the initiation of an intervention. In the absence of countercontrol from clients, institution staff will tend to design interventions in response to the current contingencies on their own behavior, including their own values. Thus, when clients always or at least some of the time do not participate in the design of the intervention, their rights should be protected by inclusion of special mechanisms that give other individuals the reinforcers necessary to exercise countercontrol on behalf of the clients. None of the mechanisms discussed in this chapter is without its problems; each is an approximation that attempts to provide protections otherwise lacking.

FIVE

Schools

When behavior modification was first introduced, schoolteachers, like the staffs of institutions, responded to it as a possible answer to long-standing problems of motivating their students. Behavioral technology was found to produce dramatic improvements in classroom management (O'Leary and O'Leary, 1972), at least initially. With success came doubts; critics raised a variety of charges regarding presumed ill effects and side effects of the use of behavior modification in the schools. To the extent that those issues are related to ethical questions, they will be dealt with in this chapter.

The chapter is based on three sources: case studies that the commission conducted of ongoing behavior modification programs in school settings, a review of the relevant behavioral literature, and discussions between commission members and professionals involved in the application of behavior modification in schools.

Identification of the Client

We have distinguished in this report between two senses of the term *client:* (1) the person whose behavior is to be changed and (2) the person offering reinforcers like pay for employment, for the psychologist's behavior. In the case of interventions in schools, the children are the clients in the first sense of this term, because change in their behavior is typically the goal of the interventions. The other sense of *client* can refer to the children's parents and also to the children's teachers, the school administrators, and the local school board.

Although the children have not hired the psychologist and are not clients in that sense, it is their behavior that the intervention is designed to modify, and, to the degree that their abilities allow, they can participate in the selection of the goals and methods of the program. Pragmatically, if the children consent to participate in a mutually agreed-on behavior program, countercontrol is likely to be minimized. Also, the children can make a meaningful contribution to the program plans by indicating preferred incentives or even suggesting different approaches.

In some sense, children normally give or withhold their consent to the regular programs in their classrooms. This is not done in any formal way, but certainly children do refuse to participate in scheduled learning tasks, and they receive whatever consequences are programmed for noncooperation, such as loss of recess time, poor grades, or failing a class. When a behavior modification program is proposed for a classroom, children should have no less right to agree or refuse to agree to participate, given that they are the clients of that program.

When a teacher recommends a special program that would be instituted for only a few children in a given class, such a recommendation needs to be based on data demonstrating that a problem exists. The data should show that those children's behavior is seriously different from behavior considered necessary for learning to occur in the classroom. The children who would be involved in that program should, if possible, be involved in its planning and give their consent to participation; their parents and the school officials also should be involved in the development of plans for a special program.

Overall, however, programs for the classroom are planned by the school officials and teachers, acting with the parents' consent. Citizens of the community delegate to the local school board the responsibility for overseeing both the normal and the innovative programs used in classrooms.

Definition of the Problem and Selection of Goals

Optimally, the target behaviors of intervention programs in the schools would be of both short-term and long-term benefit to the children. Behaviors of long-term value would be those that would continue to be supported by reinforcement from the natural environment, both in and out of school. Unfortunately, no data exist that can tell us what behaviors are of even short-term benefit for the children, and society has come to no general agreement on what represents long-term value.

As a consequence, selection of goals for programs in the classroom must be based on the hunches of those involved with the program as to what would be most beneficial for the children involved. In the absence of external criteria, those making the decisions often select as targets those behaviors that would be most reinforcing to them. For example, teachers tend to select behaviors for the children that will enable the teachers to maintain control over their classrooms. After a review of some of the early behavior modification work in "relatively normal" classrooms in public schools, Winett and Winkler (1972, p. 501) concluded that the pupil produced by these programs was one "who stays glued to his seat and desk all day, continually looks at his teacher or his text/workbook, does not talk to or in fact look at other children, does not talk unless asked to by the teacher, hopefully does not laugh or sing (at the wrong time), and assuredly passes silently in the halls." In a reply, O'Leary (1972) disputed the accuracy of this conclusion, claimed that classrooms reviewed by Winett and Winkler were not representative of average classes, and pointed to studies that had attempted to increase academic behavior. Nonetheless, O'Leary (1972) agreed with Winett and Winkler's (1972) indictment of those classroom programs whose sole goal was to teach children to "be still, be quiet, be docile."

Good deportment in the classroom may, however, have some relationship to educational growth. If a classroom is so very disruptive that learning cannot proceed and if disruptions are so reinforcing to the children that competing reinforcers cannot be found that are strong enough to shape academic behavior, then control of deportment would seem well justified. Otherwise, however, the consensus appears to be that improvement in classroom conduct will not necessarily result in academic improvement; rather, studying skills and learning improve when they are reinforced directly (O'Leary and O'Leary, 1976).

One of the programs investigated by the commission worked first on good deportment and only later on academic behavior, because of the particular children involved, the nature of the problem, and the classroom context. In this program, Project Success Environment in the Atlanta inner-city schools (Rollins, McCandless, Thompson, and Brassell, 1974), teachers trained during the summer in the use of contingency management set about modifying conduct within their classrooms at the start of the school year. Once desired conduct, as defined in the program, was established, the emphasis shifted to the reinforcement of academic behavior, with documented success. In most instances, this shift occurred during the third week of school. Previous experience with the Project Success program had demonstrated that simply reducing social disruption and increasing task involvement did not guarantee changes in academic aptitude or achievement.

Social skills, one of the types of behavior that may be taught in a classroom behavior modification program, reflect cultural differences and involve potentially conflicting values. One of the programs the commission investigated took particular care to ensure that the goals chosen for a social-skill-training program were consistent with those of the children's parents (Filipczak, Reese, Fennell, Bass, Kent, and Gilmore, 1976). In that program, conducted in a predominantly black, inner-city school, a curriculum advisory council was established so that the program could be developed by them, in cooperation with the professionals, rather than imposed from outside. Composed of individuals concerned with community action issues and educational objectives, this group also supplied "quasi counselors" to the school in order to facilitate the behavioral program. In particular, the social skills component of the program, which had originally been developed elsewhere with white, middle-class children in another school, was modified in accordance with the needs of this different population. Professional expertise was provided for setting up behavioral programs to accomplish educational and social goals established by the school staff and the community advisory committee.

As in other settings discussed in this report, psychologists working in the schools may find that their values do not coincide with those of the teachers, school administrators, or parents. O'Leary (1972), for example, has recommended that in all cases behavioral professionals should seriously evaluate whether the behavior they are being asked to change should in fact be changed. Psychologists in the schools, recognizing a conflict between their values and those of others, might attempt to influence the authorities to view the situation differently and adopt an alternative course of action or might refuse to implement a program that conflicts with their values.

Selection of the Intervention Method

The procedures whereby intervention methods are selected for use with schoolchildren are much like those for selection of the goals of the program; the main points have already been covered in the preceding subsection. However, some of the interventions used in connection with classroom programs raise special problems not yet considered in this report.

Home-Based Consequences

A type of reinforcement program widely used in classrooms is the report card or home-based contingency method. Tokens are dispensed at school, and the backup reinforcers are administered by the parents at home. The tokens are usually notes from the teacher detailing behavioral ratings on criterion behaviors (which may vary, as in any other positive reinforcement program). An obvious advantage for teachers is that the mechanics of their job are considerably simplified.

Effective use of this system depends heavily on the parents applying reinforcers in a consistent, contingent, and cooperative manner. Accordingly, the parents should be evaluated with respect to their capacity and motivation to carry out this type of program successfully. For example, a report card that is potentially unfavorable should not be used with parents who have abused their child. The psychologist must be alert to other possible adverse consequences for the child as a result of formal parental involvement in the behavior modification program. All report card procedures should be carefully monitored, not only to ensure effective operation but also to detect any untoward side effects for the child. If there is any indication that the method is unsuitable, it should be abandoned, and only classroom reinforcement procedures should be used.

Group-Oriented Reinforcement Programs

Individually scheduled contingencies for different children are often impractical if not impossible to implement (Bushell, Wrobel, and Michaelis, 1968). A practical alternative is to use group-oriented procedures. Before the introduction of behavior modification, teachers long used such procedures; for example, in spelling, athletics, and other contests where individual performance has group consequences. Several types of group-oriented classroom contingencies have been developed within behavior modification (see Litow and Pumroy, 1975; O'Leary and O'Leary, 1976), such as where the performance of one or more selected group members results in consequences for the whole group or where the performance of each member of the group must reach some standard in order for the group as a whole to be reinforced.

Drabman, Spitalnik, and Spitalnik (1974), for example, demonstrated that a group contingency token program in which group reward was determined by the behavior of a single, randomly chosen child, required the least teacher time and was the teacher's preferred method, compared to individual contingencies and other group-oriented programs. On the whole, group-oriented contingencies have been shown to be as effective, if not more effective, than individual rewards delivered contingent on individual performance (Litow and Pumroy, 1975).

Group-oriented programs have been criticized for improperly and unfairly using nonproblem children to influence the behavior of problem children. Group-oriented contingencies may even be detrimental to positive interpersonal relations among the children. Axelrod (1973), for example, found that a group contingency resulted in peer pressure in the form of verbal threats, which themselves were a source of classroom disruption. O'Leary and Drabman (1971, p. 390), in cautioning about the use of group-oriented contingencies, point out that one or two children might find it reinforcing to "subvert the program or 'beat the system.' " And, if the target children are unable to perform the requisite criterion behavior, they will be placed under pressure they can do nothing to avoid.

Martin (1972) has questioned the legality of group contingency programs. Contending that group pressure might interfere with the "psychological well-being" of a student, Martin suggests that the Fifth and Fourteenth Amendment clauses concerning the right to life, liberty, and property can be construed to imply the right to "psychological integrity." He makes the point that although behavioral psychologists are responsible for the consequences of a group contingency program, they cannot control precisely the level of pressure exerted by some of the children in the class on other children. Martin (1972, p. 57) recommends that this type of group-oriented procedure be used only in "severe situations where traditional methods fail and where the teacher makes special efforts to control the severity of the pressure."

On the whole, the use of group-oriented programs, like individual programs, must be monitored for potentially undesirable side effects, as well as to provide data demonstrating their effectiveness.

Side Effects of Programs Using Tangible Reinforcers

On the basis of the overjustification hypothesis (Lepper, Green, and Nisbett, 1973), token reinforcement programs have been criticized on the grounds that the extrinsic reinforcers may undermine children's intrinsic interest in the activities for which they are being reinforced (Levine and Fasnacht, 1974). This argument has generated considerable controversy. Empirically, the general claim that extrinsic rewards undermine intrinsic interest does not seem to agree with the bulk of the data (Feingold and Mahoney, 1975).

Furthermore, with respect to behavioral programs using token economies in the classroom, what little support there is for the undermining effect of extrinsic reward on subsequent interest seems to be limited to a narrow set of circumstances. The Levine and Fasnacht (1974) argument was predicated on the use of external reinforcers for behaviors already at high rate. In actual practice, token economies differ considerably from the conditions that characterized the studies showing the negative effect on interest (see Feingold and Mahoney, 1975). Rarely would tokens be given for high-rate behavior. Moreover, studies of token economies that have included follow-up data typically report that, even in those instances where the behavioral improvement observed while the token program was in effect dissipated after an abrupt withdrawal of tokens, the behavior did not deteriorate to a level worse than the pretreatment baseline (Ford and Foster, 1976).

Other Issues Related to Tangible Reinforcers

To promote generalization of behavior change to the non-token economy classroom, token systems in the classroom probably should be eliminated gradually, while at the same time, social reinforcers and reinforcers intrinsic to the performance of the tasks become effective consequences. In behavioral programs reported in the literature, the tangible reinforcers have not always been removed as quickly as it might have been possible to do so. More recent programs tend to remove the extrinsic reinforcers sooner than did programs developed in the early days of behavior modification.

Recently, also, there has been a trend away from the use of tangible rewards like candy, trinkets, and money and toward reinforcers more naturally available in the classroom, like extra recess, special activities, and privileges (O'Leary and O'Leary, 1976). Earlier programs seemed to use artificial reinforcers even when milder, more natural means would probably have been effective (Wexler, 1973).

An often expressed concern is whether a token program applied selectively to some target children in a classroom might have adverse effects on the nontarget children. More specifically, critics have suggested that the latter may feel deprived or perhaps even may behave badly in order to obtain reinforcers themselves. The schools the commission studied experienced little difficulty with children who were not participating in special programs; they attributed this to the effective way in which the teachers and principals explained the programs to the children. In one school, for example, both target and nontarget children participated in some reinforcing activity at the end of the week, with the target children regarded by the others as needing greater attention because of their educational deficits. An empirical analysis of the behavior of the target and nontarget children in one such study (Christy, 1975) showed that the nontarget children did not behave any worse while the target children were being reinforced and that their behavior actually improved somewhat over the course of the study. Although the nontarget children initially complained that they did not receive the reinforcers, the complaints gradually stopped.

The converse of this situation is that nontarget children may actually show improved behavior. A small but growing body of literature suggests that, in at least some circumstances, children whose peers are receiving reinforcers may demonstrate improvement in the absence of a special program for their own behavior (for example, see Strain, Shores, and Kerr, 1976).

On the whole, token programs appear to offer a valuable aid in developing children's academic and social competence. Praise and grades have long been used in the schools. Token programs are only slightly different and do not seem to be either more severe or more restrictive. Although long-term data on the effects of extrinsic reinforcers like tokens are lacking, the data available suggest that a program begin by using reinforcers available in the classroom prior to the introduction of special consequences.

Accountability

A behavior modification program requires extensive involvement on the part of behavior change agents, continuous monitoring, and frequent reevaluation in the light of the data. Many a program once effective has subsequently collapsed and disappeared with the departure of the original investigator. Quality control thus involves the maintenance of successful programs once the professionals, usually acting as temporary outside consultants, leave.

An important practical consideration which has to be faced is that when teachers engage in behavior modification programs, or any special program, extra time and effort are required. Reinforcers must be provided to maintain this additional activity, just as pupils receive reinforcers for their appropriate behavior. Drabman and Tucker (1974) observe that token programs fail when the teachers implementing them do not want them. Ample evidence shows that change in the pupils' behavior alone is seldom sufficient to reinforce their teachers' performance. Financial rewards for teachers for extra efforts in behavioral programs have been suggested, but such a policy is unlikely to be widely used because of difficulties in measuring behavior change and because of budgetary problems and possible opposition from teacher organizations (Brown, 1976; Martin, 1974). Yet bonus payments might be necessary to change teacher behavior effectively; the procedure could be adjusted to accommodate the established practices in the schools (Harris, Bushell, Sherman, and Kane, 1975).

Another alternative would be to have the principal, assistant principal, or elementary supervisor recognize the teachers' efforts. An example of how this can be accomplished is furnished by the Project Success Environment (Rollins and others, 1974). Noting that there is broad agreement among educators that the principal is ultimately responsible for determining how or if students learn, especially in elementary classrooms, Rollins and others (1974) describe an intervention program designed to be managed by a single administrator, the principal. A striking impression from one of our case studies was that the energetic and enthusiastic involvement and constructive support of the principal contributed to the generally favorable climate among pupils, teachers, and professionals at the school.

Protection of the Client's Rights

Even preschool children might be competent to understand a suitably simple explanation of a proposed program; therefore, psychologists should consider attempting to obtain consent from them. Certainly, children involved in a special program should be able to demonstrate that they understand what the program is about and that they know how to withdraw from the program, should they not want to continue to participate in it.

In one of the schools examined as a case study, the students and their parents were fully informed about the program being offered and had several opportunities for entering and leaving the program. In practice, most of these options related directly to actions by the parents rather than by the child. Beginning with the first contact, the parents were encouraged to discuss the program with their child and come to a mutually agreed-on decision about participating. Only the parents' signature was formally required on the permission letter sent to the project. The children had the right to ask their counselor to let them withdraw from the program. The children could also ask their parents for support for withdrawing from the classes.

In either instance, however, their desire to withdraw had to be transmitted through their parents. It was not necessary for the parents to concur strongly with the request, only to know of and understand it. The request for termination could be made of the principal, a teacher, a counselor, or the behavioral psychologist. These options for termination were always open to students and their parents. The procedure also offered a due-process mechanism whereby program participants could express discontent and grievances (Filipczak and Friedman, in press).

Ethical Issues in Behavior Modification

As in all other special education programs, administrators of behavior modification programs have problems in getting consent from parents who are frequently absent from their homes or uninterested in special programs for their children. In some cases, community workers can personally contact parents who do not respond to notes sent home with their children.

Special care should be taken when consent is being obtained for programs in which whole classes are involved or where group contingencies will be used, to ensure that one parent or child or a very small number who refuse are not subjected to negative social sanctions from the group that does participate. Alternative activities might be made available for children not participating in the group program.

Summary and Conclusions

Special intervention programs conducted in classrooms share common problems in relation to consent and the selection of target behavior. The problem of obtaining consent from children is compounded by the fact that the psychologist conducting the intervention is not being hired by the children who will participate in it. Children's consent to the standard programs in a classroom is typically obtained implicitly, by virtue of their continued cooperation; consent to special programs like behavior modification should be obtained explicitly from the children, as well as from their parents or the school's principal. The target behavior emphasized in behavior modification programs in the past was improvement in deportment; only recently has academic achievement begun to be included as an essential aspect of the outcome of a classroom intervention. No data exist that demonstrate which classes of behavior are important or essential for schoolchildren to have; for the various alternatives possible, those selecting the goals of a program should specify the consequences for their behavior and the children's, including their values.

SIX

Prisons

This chapter and the next one are based on the commission's case studies of the use of behavior modification in prisons. For the purposes of this report, we assume as given society's right to use prisons to punish, prevent, deter, and also rehabilitate those who have committed crimes. We will not address general questions such as what the role of prisons in society should be and whether prisons are the optimal way to deal with particular social problems. Rather, these two chapters of the report are concerned with the ethical implications of the use of behavior modification and other psychological interventions to achieve society's goals for prisons.

Our report on behavior modification in prisons consists of two parts. This first chapter is descriptive, its concern being to give a reasonably complete outline of ethical and legal issues that have been raised in connection with the use of behavior modification in prisons. In the next chapter, criticisms are mentioned, and a detailed argument is presented for one point of view. We do not expect that everyone will be convinced by the argument. Its thrust is that, given what is known about behavior, behavior modification programs in prisons should be reevaluated and redesigned with different methods and different goals.

The programs discussed in this section, both actual and ideal, are associated with closed prisons—that is, total institutions. Nothing in these two chapters necessarily applies to programs conducted in open settings, such as halfway houses.

Identification of the Client

In all the cases investigated, the clients—the parties with whom the psychologist negotiated goals and procedures—were the prison authorities. In no case did the prisoners participate fully in the negotiation of goals and procedures. In many cases, they did not even help decide whether they would enter and remain in the program. In some cases, the prisoners' suggestions were solicited and considered; in some, details of the program, such as specific educational goals, were negotiated with the prisoners and formalized in behavioral contracts. That the program would have educational goals was, however, decided by the prison authorities. It might be contended, nevertheless, that the prisoners were the clients, in the sense that they were the parties whose interests and needs were met by the program.

Definition of the Problem and Selection of Goals

The problem to be dealt with in a prison setting can be defined in different ways, and this leads to the development of different types of goals and different remedial programs.

To Control Difficult Prisoners

Some prisoners are regarded as especially prone to cause trouble, to breed violence and dissent, and to provoke revolt. These prisoners are said to be extremely difficult to manage in conventional prisons; they seriously disrupt the management of the prison. They are said to be unable or unwilling to adhere to established regulations, to be disruptive, and to exhibit behavior detrimental to their own and other prisoners' welfare and adjustment and detrimental to the integrity of the prison. According to the handbook of one prison program, such prisoners "are usually characterized as inmates who adhere completely to the criminal value system and its norms." When the problem is so defined, the major goal is that, in a reasonably short period of time (usually four to eighteen months), these prisoners will no longer exhibit this undesirable behavior when incarcerated in a conventional prison.

Some programs have additional goals related to this general one. One program, for example, diagnosed the undesirable behavior as a function of the reinforcement contingencies operative within the "inmate peer culture" and set the goal of disrupting that culture so as to alter the reinforcement contingencies. That program also proposed to change the prisoners' values as measured by semantic differential tests.

To Do Research on Interventions

Conventional prisons manage and control prisoners primarily through punitive techniques. Researchers have attempted to determine experimentally whether the effectiveness of such techniques can be matched or bettered by techniques that employ only positive reinforcement, such as a token economy. The immediate goal is to develop an effective technology; the long-term goal is to replace punitive controls by positive ones in prison management.

Although the fundamental goals of programs aimed at controlling difficult prisoners and programs devoted to research differ, they share specific behavioral targets. These are, for the most part, laid down by the prison authorities and are the same goals that most conventional prisons have. Typically, they concern such matters as punctuality, personal cleanliness, work tasks, speech (no abuse, cursing, or foul language), interaction with prison personnel (proper politeness and mode of address, obeying orders, and ready acceptance of denials of requests) and with other prisoners (no disruptions or agitations), and educational activities. The educational activities rarely occupy a large part of a prisoner's daily life; the remaining goals relate primarily to institutional management and involve behavior characterized by nonassertiveness, submissiveness, and docility.

To Eliminate Specific Behavior

Some prisoners have exhibited unacceptable and socially repulsive behavior, such as child molesting or other violations of society's sexual norms. Thus a third type of goal is to eliminate such behavior; some programs state a related goal: to eliminate any associated fantasies.

To Rehabilitate the Prisoners

All prison programs claim a further goal, rehabilitation. In no case, however, is rehabilitation a separately programmed goal. Rather, it appears to be claimed that programs will achieve this goal concurrently with their other goals.

Types of Special Programs

These various definitions of the problem and the associated goals lead to significant differences in programs.

Total Programs

Total programs for difficult prisoners isolate them in a special institution where their behavior is to be changed. The program applies throughout the day and affects almost every detail of the prisoners' activity. The design of the program incorporates many ingredients of behavior modification systems developed in other types of institutions; for example, reinforcers are arranged to be delivered following specific behaviors, and there is a carefully graded progression of behavioral criteria for reinforcement. The following is a description of one quite typical program of this type (Holland, 1975), albeit a program that has been discontinued.

This total program, described as a "status system," contained three stages or tiers. These stages were subdivided into nine levels, identifying different deprivation conditions. Promotion to higher levels depended on meeting a series of criteria. The entering prisoner began at the bottom level, where he relinquished all personal property. He was kept in isolation and had almost no privileges—only a bed, mattress, pillow, and a minimum of toilet articles. He could shower and change clothes twice weekly. He ate in his cell, where he was locked most of the time. He had no visitors, no personal reading material, and no radio. He could not use the commissary or have cigarettes. From this rather severe condition of privation, he had to earn his way up through the stages.

Level two allowed slightly better conditions, such as a very limited commissary privilege and an increase in showers to three times a week. In the upper levels, conditions were much better. The prisoner was allowed to visit the library and had a full-time assignment in the prison industry. He could subscribe to approved newspapers or magazines and had a commissary privilege of up to $15 a month, depending on the points he earned. He could shower and change clothes daily.

A rather carefully worked-out system of reinforcement contingencies was used to provide points that defined a currency in the token economy, where they could be exchanged for the purchase of goods, the rental of radios and books, and so on. Points were earned for personal appearance and personal hygiene, for individualized learning programs, for work tasks in the prison industry, and for numerous adaptive social interactions involving obedience and passivity.

Promotion between levels was also dependent on a set of contingencies summarized in what was called a "good day" score. A specified number of successive good days entitled the prisoner to promotion to a higher level on review of the staff. There were clearly specified behavioral criteria recorded each day by the staff to determine a "good day." The "good day" criteria included especially heavy emphasis on general submission to the authority of the guards. For example, one criterion was that the prisoner "accepted or performed assignments, duties, or tasks without needing persuasion" (U.S. Congress, 1974b, p. 267). Others were that the prisoner followed directions and instructions in a willing manner without bickering; followed rules, regulations, and policies of the unit; communicated with others in a reasonable tone of voice without belittling, agitating, or using abusive language; accepted a "no" or a reasonable response when making requests; and made requests in a nonabusive manner (Holland, 1975).

The program mentioned earlier that sought to change values and disrupt the inmate peer culture also included another feature: The prisoners were required to participate in guided group interaction sessions. These sessions were conceived as thoroughly integrated with the operant conditioning-based conception of the total program. They were part of the token economy; they played a role in the dispensing of reinforcers; an attempt was made to analyze the interactions among the participants in terms of categories derived from operant conditioning; and the sessions addressed themselves to individual behaviors, including verbal behavior.

All the total programs we investigated included an explicit role for punishment. Points could be lost, and the prisoner demoted to earlier stages, for certain behaviors or for failure to perform certain tasks.

Research-Oriented Programs

Research-oriented programs, at least the ones attempted to date, do not aim to be total. In some cases, they apply only in the prisoners' nonworking hours. They are less intrusive into the prisoners' behavior. The programs do not involve stages with differing access to reinforcers or degrees of deprivation. In a prison token economy, as in other uses of this method, tokens are awarded for specified behaviors and then may be exchanged for backup reinforcers. Initially, the prisoners participating in such a program are not significantly more deprived than other inmates of the prison. There may be some initial deprivation, in which the prisoners in the research program are denied time in the prison at large and access to certain recreational areas; tokens can then be used to purchase time and access. These programs involve no programmed punishment except for loss of tokens charged for violating conditions of the token economy.

Treatment-Oriented Programs

These programs aim to provide treatment for a restricted set of behaviors and do not establish a detailed set of contingencies of reinforcement that control a major proportion of the prisoners' daily behavior. Rather, they are quite similar in form to the style of therapy engaged in by the private practitioner in one-to-one or group therapeutic sessions. The programs often involve the use of aversive conditioning or covert sensitization, and typically they deal with individuals' crime-related behavior. The programs differ from those of the private practitioner in that the clients are prisoners.

The evidence for successful behavior change in these programs is limited. Whether the sexual practices of the pedophile, for example, are greatly changed by giving him an electric shock while he looks at pictures of children—as was done in one of the case studies—is not known. In general, the prisoners' verbal statements concerning a lack of further interest in pictures of children serve both as the basis for the men's release and for reports on treatment effectiveness.

Because these programs require a high ratio of staff professionals to prisoners, the economics of prisons limits their use.

Accountability

In almost all cases, the personnel of the program are directly accountable only to the prison authorities. In some research-oriented programs, the planners are responsible to funding agencies, and they often submit their plans to the judgment of a federal review panel or a local citizens' review committee. All psychologists are, of course, ultimately accountable to their profession and to society for adhering to the ethics code of their profession.

Quality of Staff and Staff Training

All the programs used as case studies were designed and usually overseen by behavioral psychologists with standard credentials. Both the total and the research-oriented programs included some emphasis on the training of prison personnel in behavior modification principles and practice, with a strong emphasis on positive reinforcement.

A problem that might derive from inadequately trained staff was the fear common among prisoners that behavior modification programs involve treatments like lobotomy. Adequate preparation of the prison population for a new program might have avoided such misperceptions and allayed this and similar fears.

Quality of the Intervention

Almost all the programs examined as case studies were based on behavioral principles and used behavior modification techniques tested in other settings, such as schools and mental hospitals. One exception is the program that incorporated group interaction sessions, which are not behaviorally based. In some programs, the design originally planned and explained to the prisoners could not be implemented because of serious failures of cooperation on the part of prison authorities. As far as we could determine, none of the total programs was preceded by a detailed behavioral assessment, based on extended observations, of the contingencies prevailing in the prison.

Record Keeping and Confidentiality

In some prison systems, psychologists' records and reports can be a factor in the granting of parole. Especially in those cases where a prisoner is serving a sentence of indeterminate length, this can raise serious concerns. However, the confidentiality of records in prisons is not a special problem for behavior modification, and so it will not be considered further here.

Protection of the Prisoners' Rights

Potential threats to the prisoners' rights and means for safeguarding them from those threats will be considered in this section. Because of the emphasis in this book on the use of behavior modification in practice, rather than in research, issues of protection for prisoners participating in research-oriented programs will not be discussed here, for the most part. This topic is, in itself, an enormously complex one and is treated at length in the report of the National Commission for the Protection of Human Subjects of Biomedical and Behavioral Research (1976). In brief, the National Commission recommends that programs involving research on interventions in prisons be conducted only if the investigators are competent, the research facilities are adequate, and the research has been reviewed by a committee which has considered the risks involved, the provisions for obtaining informed consent, the safeguards to protect the prisoners' dignity and confidentiality, the procedures for the selection of subjects for the research, and the provisions for providing compensation for research-related injuries. The report specifies in some detail the composition of the review committee, including prisoners or prisoner advocates and community representatives. Because the issues surrounding research programs in prisons have been taken up in such depth by the National Commission, the following discussion will be confined to total programs and treatment-oriented programs.

Informed Consent

In the total programs examined in connection with the case studies, informed consent by the prisoners was wholly lacking. Typically, in these programs, the prisoners were transferred to the site of the program following orders from the prison authorities. Once on the site of the special program, participation in the program was coerced by making the alternative to cooperation solitary confinement in extremely deprived (and, according to prisoners' reports, harassing) conditions.

Informed consent appeared to be more carefully obtained in the treatment-oriented programs we examined. In most of these programs, participants signed a consent form. However, even so, questions can be seriously raised regarding whether their consent was informed and uncoerced. It is an open issue whether requiring participation in treatment as a condition for early release is permissible on due-process grounds. In practice, this subtly coercive contingency is often used, and alternative forms of treatment are rarely available.

If informed consent is to be uncoerced, the prisoners must be in a position to consent or refuse to consent, with no differential consequences. Informed consent also requires that the prisoners be given in advance a detailed account of the procedure; this is usually done. In addition, the prisoners should be told the consequences of the procedure, the likelihood that the problem behavior will be eliminated inside and outside the prison, and the advantages and disadvantages of the proposed program in comparison with other procedures.

Due Process

At the time the case studies were conducted, court decisions had held that a hearing was required before prisoners could be transferred involuntarily to another prison or if prisoners' situation were to change so that they would be deprived for a long time of important privileges otherwise enjoyed by inmates (Friedman, 1975). In some cases in the prison programs we examined, it was alleged that such a hearing was not held.

Use of Punishment

Punishment is, of course, in the nature of prisons, which are designed to remove individuals from the reinforcers of everyday life.

Issues relevant here have to do with the addition of special punishments associated with behavior modification programs.

In behavioral terms, both the presentation of an aversive consequence and the withdrawal of a positive reinforcer function as punishment when the responses that these events follow decrease in frequency in the future. Not everything aversive is punishing, of course; a common example of a nonpunishing aversive event is a painful medical procedure. In order for a punishment to be effective in controlling the future emission of a given behavior, the punishment should be contingent on that behavior. Punishment delivered to individuals independently of their behavior may lead to aggression or to an overall decrease in activity, rather than to a selective decrease in a particular behavior or class of responses.

In regular prisons, solitary confinement is used as punishment for various offenses, such as violent disruptive behavior; its imposition requires a hearing. In behavioral programs in prisons, solitary confinement for an indefinite period is sometimes used as a punishment for refusing to participate in the program or for failure to meet certain demands of the program. In the programs we investigated, this punishment was applied routinely without a hearing. Another punishment used in behavioral programs is return to the initial state, where few reinforcers were available.

In all the total programs we examined, prisoners had reported the routine use of unprogrammed punishment. Often these punishments were particularly ugly, including prisoners being shackled, urine being mixed into the prison food, or vomit-inducing or paralyzing drugs being administered. Unprogrammed punishment, as well as punishment for the purpose of maintaining order in the prison or obtaining revenge, should be distinguished from punishment that is designed to be part of a systematic program for treatment purposes. Furthermore, informed consent is especially critical when punishment procedures are to be used.

In some prison programs in the recent past, paralytic drugs like succinylcholine chloride (Anectine) have been used essentially noncontingent on specific behaviors; these procedures have been labeled as behavior modification. Court decisions have found such procedures to be unconstitutional in the absence of informed consent

(Friedman, 1975). On the whole, the courts have not permitted the use of "unreasonable" punishment for rule violation, but they have permitted quite drastic interventions for the temporary control of prisoners when the safety of other prisoners is threatened.

Protection of Prisoners' Privacy

The basic attitude and value changes attempted in some of the programs are possible only if contingencies can be arranged for attitudes and values. This cannot be done if attitudes and values remain privately held. For uncooperative prisoners, then, the goals can only be achieved by violating their privacy. One system planned twenty-four-hour television surveillance of the cells, until prevented from doing so by court action. Even so, in most total programs, direct surveillance is attempted.

Right to Refuse Treatment or Rehabilitation

The prison programs we examined as case studies did not recognize that the prisoners had a right to refuse to participate in the proposed treatment or refuse to be rehabilitated. Whatever the legal status of this right may be, it is certainly closely related to the topic of informed consent, discussed earlier. Note that this issue can arise even in programs where issues of due process, cruel and unusual punishment, and invasion of privacy are not present, such as in a program with the intended benign features of positive reinforcement. It can arise whenever the program includes among its goals treatment, rehabilitation, or preparation for living in another environment. It does not arise if a program is conceived as entirely custodial.

Right to Treatment

Nothing in the preceding paragraphs of this section implies that behavioral programs or other procedures should not be available to any prisoner who agrees to participate in them. Although the right of prisoners to education, training, and other programs is not generally recognized by the courts, they should have access to programs that would enhance the quality of their life after release or that would reduce the possibility of a socially unacceptable crime like child molestation being committed.

Evidence for the Efficacy of These Programs

Are the different types of prison programs appropriately designed for attaining their various goals? Is there experimental evidence supporting their use?

There is no clear evidence that total programs can achieve their goals. No program of this type to date has incorporated anything approaching adequate experimental controls in its design. It is noteworthy and shocking that the careful research so characteristic of most applied behavior analysis is absent from most prison applications of behavioral procedures. Moreover, the discrepancies between the program planned and actual practice, as evidenced, for example, by the frequency of nonprogrammed punishment, preclude the possibility of testing under existing conditions the effectiveness of the programs originally designed. A comparison of the program handbooks with prisoners' accounts of actual practice is illuminating. The prisoners' accounts emphasize the presence of nonprogrammed punishment, which they perceive—all rhetoric aside—as an essential part of the punishment to which they are being submitted.

Experimental programs that are research oriented cannot provide relevant evidence about total programs, given the important differences between the two types of programs. The research-oriented programs, dealing only with volunteers, do not need "stages" within the token economy, nor do they need an initial state of deprivation. Success in achieving comparable goals with formally similar programs in other total institutions, such as mental institutions, is insufficient evidence, given the many differences between prisons and prison inmates and the other institutions and their inmates.

The psychological principles underlying behavior modification suggest that behavior is predominantly under the control of the prevailing contingencies of reinforcement—that is, the consequences of the behavior—and of the environment in which the behavior occurs—that is, the antecedents to the behavior. Special prisons where total programs are run are different in many respects from conventional prisons, and the contingencies prevailing in those two environments differ as well. To the extent that these factors are markedly different, generalization from one setting to the other will be attenuated, and the patterns of behavior exhibited in the total program in the special prison would not carry over into the conventional one. The more similar the two prisons are, the greater will be the carryover. One way to maximize such similarity would be to design a maintenance program for the regular prison; none of the programs we investigated included one, however. Also, if the total program at the special prison included severe punishment, then prisoners would presumably act in the regular prison in whatever way is required to avoid returning to the special one. Special programs are not supposed to be severely punitive, of course.

Summary and Conclusions

This chapter has described the ethical and legal issues related to the use of behavior modification in prisons. The limitations on rights inherent in incarceration impact on behavior modification programs as much as on all other aspects of the prisoners' environment. Thus, problems exist in prisons with respect to informed consent, the selection of intervention methods and goals, and so on; the prisoners' access to reinforcers for the behavior of those conducting the programs is at most minimal, virtually eliminating the opportunity for realistic countercontrol.

The next chapter goes beyond the descriptive to a critical analysis of the use of behavior modification in prisons.

SEVEN

A Critique of the Use of Behavior Modification in Prisons

The preceding chapter described some forms of behavior modification programs in prisons and analyzed them in terms of the same major ethical issues referred to in the other chapters of this report. In addition to that form of analysis, behavior modification programs in prisons can be criticized on two other levels. The first of these deals with problems that arise in specific details of the implementation of programs; the second, more broadly, with problems that arise in relation to the goals and assumptions of the programs.

Problems in Implementation

Prison programs, whether behavior modification or some other type of program, raise special issues. Critics have charged that programs in prisons do not promote rehabilitation and have further argued that such programs should not be described as treatment, either. The adequacy of the programs offered has been questioned, and whether it is possible to obtain informed consent from prisoners is a thorny issue. These topics will be taken up in this chapter.

Do Prison Programs Promote Rehabilitation?

Prisoners are said to be rehabilitated if they cease to behave criminally after their release. That is, society's goals for former criminals are achieved if, simply, former criminals are criminals no longer. From the point of view of the prisoners, an important aspect of successful rehabilitation may be that their lives are more reinforcing and contain fewer aversive events. Rehabilitation, then, may involve procedures designed to reduce the future probability of criminal acts and also to increase the range of socially acceptable ways that the prisoners might obtain reinforcement. Ideally, the latter could include training in job-finding, on-the-job social skills, prerequisite academic skills, and skills necessary for particular vocations. Another area in which a positive rehabilitation program could provide training would be in the productive use of leisure time; that is, skills that could later be exercised in the former prisoners' home environments and that would be supported by those environments. Success in rehabilitation is usually measured by decline in the rate of recidivism; improvement in quality of life, of course, is difficult to measure.

In any case, rehabilitation programs within prisons should be linked with stages of rehabilitation outside the prison after discharge. Much research in behavior modification has shown that generalization from an artificial training situation has to be supported, at least temporarily, by an explicit program in the natural environment (Stokes and Baer, 1977).

All the prison programs investigated as part of our case-study analysis included rehabilitation among their goals, whether or not they were considered to be treatment programs. One of the programs we examined (Milan, Wood, Williams, Rogers, Hampton, and McKee, 1974) aimed to contribute toward rehabilitation by removing factors that were thought to increase recidivism and minimize the chance of rehabilitation. The program therefore emphasized the development of educational and technical skills. The hope was that a former prisoner having these skills would be able to function better in society and obtain work. These are modest and, up to a point, realistic goals, although when our economy is tolerating a very high rate of unemployment, work opportunities are a function of more than just having the appropriate educational and technical skills.

Other programs conceive of themselves as establishing in the prisoners patterns of behavior that will carry over into their life outside the prison, patterns allegedly incompatible with criminal acts. Most of these programs do not include systematic postrelease follow-up. Little evidence suggests that these programs are effective in decreasing recidivism, and evidence available from research in other areas, as already noted, suggests that the probability of carryover of behaviors learned in prison is low in the absence of a carefully designed follow-up program.

A particular problem in dealing with the criminal acts themselves is that the criminal behavior does not occur in the prison, except where it involves drug addiction, interpersonal aggression, or some sexual behaviors. As a result, a program attempting to reduce the frequency of criminal behavior that has occurred in the past can deal only with those crime-related variables that can be dealt with in the prison setting. Such programs would have enhanced effectiveness if coupled with follow-up services when the prisoner has been released to the community.

The goal of many prison programs is to produce, arbitrarily and to an excessive degree, obedience, submissiveness, docility, and passivity among the prisoners. The total programs we investigated, for example, appeared to be devoted to controlling or "treating" the violent, disruptive, noncooperative behavior of the prisoners in the programs. From the point of view of prison administrators, the prison would run more smoothly if all prisoners were passive and obedient. With such goals, the prisoner does not appear to be the real beneficiary of the program. Were the passive, obedient, submissive, and docile behaviors to generalize to settings the prisoners would be in after their release, such behaviors do not seem to be particularly adaptive or likely to enhance the quality of the former inmates' lives, especially if the passivity and obedience are carried to any extreme.

The question has arisen as to whether "the state has a compelling interest in reformation that is sufficient to thrust intrusive behavioral procedures on prisoners even over their competent objections" (Wexler, 1975, p. 139). Given the absence of evidence for rehabilitation and the inappropriateness of the goals of many rehabilitation programs, coerced participation in such programs cannot be justified.

Are Prison Programs "Treatment?"

In our opinion, much of the literature surrounding the design of behavioral programs implies that behavior modification programs change people's nature in some way. In contrast, a more behavioral approach would hold that what people do is a function of the setting stimuli and reinforcement contingencies prevalent at the time and of their history of reinforcement, especially in that setting. Thus, people's behavior patterns (their "nature") remain constant across environments only when the setting stimuli and reinforcement contingencies are similar across environments. Violence, for example, is presumably under the control of the current contingencies and the individual's history of reinforcement for violent behavior, especially in that setting. Thus, when prisoners act violently, appropriate targets for remediation include the conditions of the prison, the reinforcement contingencies, alternative ways of obtaining reinforcement, and the aversive nature of the environment.

The word *treatment* is essentially a medical term; from a behavioral point of view, describing interventions in prisons as treatment is a disservice to the prisoners. From a nonbehavioral point of view, on the other hand, labeling an intervention as treatment emphasizes the psychologists' helping role and stresses the prisoners' position as individuals in need of help, rather than as being bad or criminal persons. Even those espousing such a nonbehavioral viewpoint would not, however, assert that prisoners are mentally ill.

In contrast, the interests of some prison personnel lead them to see prison troublemakers as disturbed, flawed, or mentally ill and hence in need of treatment. In that conceptualization, prisoners become patients. This labeling may even inhibit the development of a professional-client relationship between the psychologist and the prisoner.

Are the Programs Adequate?

A major problem in the programs we investigated was the lack of a careful behavioral assessment and knowledge of the physical and social contingencies existing in the prisons prior to the introduction of the programs. The behavioral programs seemed designed to be analogous to programs already implemented in schools and in other total institutions, and the special sorts of contingencies existing in the prisons were not considered. This lack of analysis may explain how unprogrammed punishments came to be used; such contingencies are typical of the normal conditions in prisons.

Furthermore, the psychologists running the programs also often failed to base the programs on a behavioral assessment of the prisoners' repertoires; instead, they simply accepted the categorization of the prisoners provided by the prison authorities as a basis for decisions about program design. When this happens, the prisoners have good reason to see the psychologists as agents of the prison authorities, rather than as people interested in the prisoners' welfare.

The programs examined did not use standard, experimentally validated procedures. At best, they could be described as badly designed experiments masquerading as treatments. Intervention programs in prisons should either use only validated procedures or else be frankly and seriously experimental, and they should incorporate all the available techniques for the protection of the subjects of research.

Sometimes aversive techniques are used in prisons, on the apparent justification that they have greater long-term effectiveness than alternative techniques. Not only is there a lack of strong experimental evidence for such claims, but also aversive techniques typically seem to be reserved for use in connection with criminal behavior like child molesting that elicits moral indignation, behaviors that, as it were, invite retaliation (Holland, in press; Stolz, in press, b). Aversive techniques are not used, for example, in connection with burglary or pickpocketing. This analysis suggests that aversive techniques are selected on the basis not only of their efficacy but also of the moral stance of the administrators of the program.

Is Informed Consent Possible in Prison Programs?

In legal terms, informed consent requires that the individuals be told what a program involves, that they be competent to understand what they have been told, and that they voluntarily agree to participate in the program. Virtually all prisoners are intellectually competent to understand an explanation of a proposed program. Suppose that a careful explanation is given to them in advance—can they voluntarily choose to participate or not to participate? This is one of the thorniest questions in an ethical analysis of prison programs and a particularly difficult one to deal with from a behavioral point of view.

Offering prisoners the opportunity to participate in a treatment-oriented program in which they can participate or not, without differential consequences, seems a reasonable approach. Treatments should be available; our objection is to coerced treatments.

With respect to total programs, informed consent has in the past been lacking; prisoners have been simply assigned to the programs. It would seem possible for the prison administrators to select a group of prisoners who might benefit from a total program and then permit them to determine whether or not they participate. Leaving the decision to the individual prisoner helps to resolve the ethical problem. Prisons would then have to make the special programs sufficiently attractive that prisoners would choose to cooperate.

Persons opposed to prisons and, often, to any attempt to ameliorate conditions in prisons, have argued that psychologists should not offer any programs to prisoners, because anything that improves the conditions in prisons will postpone the day when they are eliminated entirely. However, prisons do exist, and the prisoners must live in them. The other side of the coercion issue is whether people opposed to interventions in prisons can coerce psychologists into not offering programs to prisoners. If some intervention would enhance the quality of prisoners' life after release, they should have the option of selecting or not selecting it. And if there were evidence, although there apparently is not, that some particular program would reduce the possibility of a particular crime not being committed in the future, the program should not be withheld. The prisoners should have the option of participating or not participating in it.

A Critique of the Goals and Assumptions of Prison Programs

The preceding criticisms spring from what might be called a liberal, civil libertarian perspective. Although based on behavioral principles, the criticisms presume that prisoners have rights and psychologists have duties, that it is proper for the state (and prison authorities) to lay down goals to be achieved with the inmates, and that it is proper for psychologists to lend their expertise in furthering these goals, provided that in the course of doing so the civil liberties of the prisoners are respected.

A more radical criticism of prisons—and of behavior modification programs in them—would contend that these are at best superficial criticisms that ignore the reality of what actually occurs in prisons. In this part of the chapter, we will present such a radical critique.

From a civil libertarian perspective, research-oriented programs, with their extra precautions and protections for the inmates, might seem acceptable. However, at least one serious critic (Opton, 1974, 1975) has argued that this is not so. Opton contends that any success that research-oriented programs have unintentionally gives support to practices that, in the vast majority of instances, will violate the rights of prisoners. He maintains that any thinking about prisons must recognize that in prisons whatever abuse can happen will happen. Given the goals of the programs and the nature of prisons, abuses are inevitable, according to Opton.

What has actually happened in prison programs supports Opton's contention. We mentioned earlier, for example, anecdotal reports from prisoners of the routine use of unprogrammed punishment in behavioral programs. The introduction of a novel program like a behavior modification intervention into the prisons does not, by itself, eliminate the normal contingencies in that environment. The types of contingencies that usually prevail in prisons result in a discord between the idealistic intent of a new program and actual practice. A prior behavioral assessment of the setting might enable psychologists to anticipate this kind of problem. Unfortunately, the very structure of prisons entails the use of punishment. Thus, ensuring that an innovative program does not inadvertently include the opportunity for unprogrammed punishment is a major problem.

Is it possible that there would be a time when all civil liberties issues in prisons would be satisfactorily resolved, a time when prisons are smoothly managed and are based on a technology that uses only positive controls, with guards playing only their programmed roles? In our opinion, it is not clear that there ever will be such a time. Research showing the success of positive reinforcement with volunteer subjects is not a strong basis for expecting similar success with a general prison population. It is likely that there will always be some prisoner who will resist controls and who will find intolerable the degree of surveillance and intrusion required in, for example, a token economy. If these expectations are correct, then a program involving levels or stages of deprivation and access to reinforcement—and hence the potential availability of punishment—may be essential for achieving control and conducting a successful behavior modification program in prisons.

Suppose, however, that the civil libertarian issues could be satisfactorily resolved. Ethical issues would remain at another level, and these are discussed in the remainder of this part of the book. In what follows, we will contrast a critique and analysis of existing programs, as exemplified by our case studies, with an alternative, radical position.

Who Is the Client?

Asking who the client is, in the sense of who pays the psychologist, is another way of asking who can exercise countercontrol on the psychologist's behavior. The term *client* can also refer, as we have indicated several times in the preceding chapters, to the individual whose behavior is to be modified.

Analysis of the Current Situation

The psychologist offering an intervention can be the agent of the prison authorities or the agent of the prisoners. Although these two possibilities are logically possible, in practice the psychologists' client is the prison authorities and, through them, society. This arrangement is justified on the grounds that psychologists have a duty to help society change the prisoners, in order to protect society once they are released. Assuming that prisoners have the right to refuse to participate in the programs and to refuse to change, the psychologists' duty to society requires that prisoners be offered the opportunity to change and the possibility of obtaining reinforcers that would be associated with a lowering of their future rate of criminal behavior. This justification is buttressed with the claim that it is the government's business to set goals which are then to be realized as effectively as possible by the behavior analyst.

As a result, even the most liberally designed prison programs that we investigated stopped short of accepting the prisoners as full-fledged clients who would make a major contribution to the formation of the goals of the program. Thus, in effect, prisoners are not the psychologists' clients in the same sense that people can be clients in the private practice of behavior modification. Milan and others (1974), for example, apparently accept this arrangement, but uneasily.

Those who are willing to work in an arrangement where the individuals who are to be changed are not the psychologists' clients sometimes justify this arrangement on humanitarian grounds. They argue that if the psychologists do not accept the goals laid down by prison authorities, courts, legislatures, and parole boards, they cannot have any effect on the prison structure or on the individual prisoners (for example, Hobbs and Holt, 1976; Milan and McKee, 1976).

An Alternative

An alternative position, not represented among the programs we investigated, is that the prisoners themselves should be the agents with whom goals and procedures are negotiated. More generally, in any behavior modification program, the people whose behavior is to be modified should be included when goals are being determined, assuming that they are competent to be included in such discussions.

Not including prisoners in program decisions carries the implication that they are not competent to participate, an assumption that we contend is contrary to fact. Asserting that prisoners are competent does not deny that they have exhibited behavior that our society does not accept and that may justify incarceration. However, simply because they are incarcerated for crimes does not mean that they should be treated as incompetent or that goals must be set for them.

Requiring that the prisoners be realistically involved means that they should collaborate fully in both the setting of program goals and in the detailed planning of the contingencies to be used to further those goals. Once prisoners are treated as clients and included in the preprogram decision making, coerced participation will be much less likely to occur.

What Are the Goals of the Program?

The research-oriented programs that we investigated, as well as those involving control of the total prison regimen, share most of their specific behavioral goals. They reinforce and extinguish or punish the same kinds of behavior.

Analysis of the Current Situation

Both total programs and research-oriented programs aim to produce excessively and arbitrarily docile, obedient, submissive, and passive prisoners; both manipulate the prisoners to make them behave in ways laid down by the prison authorities. The programs are designed so that the contingencies introduced will result in the occurrence of the desirable behavior.

What is the reason for manipulating the prisoners' behavior with this goal? It is widely accepted that the docile and submissive, those who accept the system no matter what their lot in it might be, are less likely to engage in criminal activity. Given such an assumption, it could be seen as reasonable to attempt to produce docility among prisoners, to use coercion if that is judged effective in changing personal defects, and to hope that the changes produced in the prisons will carry over to life after release.

We have already argued, however, that it seems spurious to claim that teaching docile and submissive behavior has anything to do with rehabilitation of the prisoners. Such a goal does not appear to be in the prisoners' long-term interest. Having docile and passive prisoners is, however, in the interest of the prison authorities and guards, because such successful control aids the smooth running of the institution. And it is not a minor factor here that it is in society's interest to maintain smoothly running prisons.

Many people feel that a major function of prisons is to separate criminals from society, in order to protect society; to punish those who have violated the law; and to deter them and others from committing future crimes. Those primarily interested in punishment and deterrence are not necessarily interested in the introduction of positive controls. Those whose major goal for prisons is to have criminals separated from society may look to applied behavior analysts for an efficient system of prison management.

It may not be inappropriate to remove individuals from the natural settings that reinforce their criminal behavior, for a period of detention, in order to teach them competing or more effective behaviors useful when they reenter their usual environment. This type of training is often done in other settings, such as in business training or even religious retreats. Rehabilitation efforts in an institution, away from the natural setting, are not, therefore, automatically doomed to failure.

Further, having behavioral programs in prisons may well be to the benefit of the prisoners. The programs emphasize positive reinforcement; the introduction of positive programs, rather than aversive or punishing controls, would make the prison environment more humane. Behavioral programs, appropriately designed, may reduce recidivism by teaching behavior useful in society at large.

An Alternative

From the point of view of a radical critique, the existing programs, as designed, make no sense if the major goal of prison programs is truly rehabilitation of the inmates. The design of those programs follows from the assumptions under which prison authorities must presently operate and from the fact that prisoners are not involved in the design of the programs.

Even if the behavior analyst sees docility as incompatible with criminal behavior and thus as a desirable goal, appropriate practice of behavior modification requires a systematic program of transition to the natural environment, after the target behavior has been learned in the prison environment. The characteristics of an effective maintenance program for former prisoners are not currently known.

It may be conjectured plausibly, however, that it would involve significant intrusion into the life of the released prisoners. The psychologist may find societal justification and approval for such intrusion because it may be that, given present societal structures and the contingencies they sustain, there is no way of reducing the crime rate short of massive intrusion into people's lives. So long as there is societal approval, there will be reinforcement available for such programs and any attendant intrusion. Ironically, society's approval may well rest on a conception of humanity and the causes of crime that considers personal traits responsible for action and personal defects the cause of antisocial behavior. Both these views are incompatible with the assumption underlying behavior modification.

In contrast, if prisoners are taken to be the clients of the psychologist and if the means and goals of interventions are negotiated with them, as we suggested earlier, then it seems likely that the only programs that will be adopted within the prisons will be those having educational or training goals. With the prisoners as clients, the applied behavior analyst would not be involved in day-to-day programs designed to smooth the running of the prisons by controlling the behavior of the prisoners; the primary concern of prison programs would be with the enhancement of the quality of life of the prisoners, especially after their release. Presumably, any program that did not further this goal would be rejected.

With a broadened sense of their clientele, psychologists would also be more concerned with prevention. Not much is known currently about how to prevent crime. However, the likelihood of prevention becoming a serious, realizable goal is increased when the contingencies that produce and maintain criminal behavior are known. Currently, there is sharp disagreement regarding which kind of factor is causally predominant—environmental contingencies or personal traits. Nevertheless, the principles underlying behavior modification can be interpreted to posit the idea that criminal behavior, like other behavior, is predominantly under the control of environmental contingencies. Concern with prevention may lead the behavioral researcher to attempt to unravel the details of such contingencies empirically and then to participate in appropriate professional action to effect relevant changes. This urgent task is present whether or not acceptable programs can be instituted in prisons.

Some Additional Comments and a Look Ahead

Real problems are present in prisons, deriving from their nature as closed institutions and from their preexisting function in the control of those who have committed crimes. The options present within the prison system are necessarily limited. If the arguments so far presented are sound, then presently conceived behavior modification programs in prisons, although they may ameliorate current practices, are either defective in their protection of the prisoners' rights or participate in the oppression of prisoners. Furthermore, when prisons have intervention programs like behavior modification, the existence of such programs can be used to disarm those who would otherwise criticize the very nature of the institution of prisons. The innovative program can be pointed to as evidence that the prison administration is working on improving the prisoners' environment. Thus psychologists working in prisons may inadvertently help to shore up the institution of prisons and postpone needed reforms.

Is there a realistic promise of future fundamental change? It is risky to hope that successful reforms will lead to a situation in which psychologists will be able to introduce more flexible programs, in which they have a professional-client relationship with the prisoners. That could happen. But success could also breed harsher programs, because if positive controls fail there may be little resistance to using harsher methods. Thus, truly fundamental change would require not only that prisoners become true parties to the negotiation of goals but also that the conception and structure of prisons be changed extensively. Fundamental change would also entail the development of programs with goals that, if achieved and maintained in society, would make it possible for the ex-prisoner to live competently, with a reasonable quality of life, without engaging in crime. Such programs may require a framework of probation and parole structures, including halfway houses and supportive group activities.

It is not obvious that these changes are possible within the present structure of society. The issues raised here are complex, and this report has ventured only a glimpse into them. According to FBI statistics, the overwhelming majority of crimes for which offenders are apprehended and imprisoned are property crimes, committed for the most part by people who are unemployed or hold low-income jobs. This is compatible with the claim that one reason that people commit crimes is to get money and material goods (see Kennedy, 1976), a claim that is surely consistent with reinforcement principles. This is supported by statistics that show that continuous employment after release from prison is the best single predictor of nonrecidivism (Glaser, 1964). Even in the absence of any additional supporting data, an analysis of the crime-related contingencies in our society suggests that the contingencies sustained by the economic structure of society are a major factor in shaping and maintaining criminal behavior.

Is it plausible that criminal behavior can be significantly reduced, without increased suppression, unless the economic structure is changed? Although the criminal behavior of some individuals may be eliminated by improving their economic lot, such as by providing decent jobs for them, the economic structure nevertheless limits the generality of this result. Without a much more detailed analysis of the social contingencies that produce crime, the possibility of relevant changes cannot be ascertained.

The principles underlying behavior modification imply that criminal behavior, like all other behavior, is largely a consequence of societal contingencies. A natural corollary of this view is that a way to eliminate crime is to change the societal contingencies. The specific changes required are yet to be discovered, however.

On the other hand, it may be possible to eliminate or markedly reduce crime by changing the details of the contingencies immediately operative on certain individuals, while maintaining the essentials of the societal contingencies unchanged. Changing the contingencies operative on an individual may involve a change in stimulus function—an aversive event is no longer aversive, something formerly neutral is now a positive reinforcer—rather than a topographic change or a change in what actually happens following the individual's behavior. If the stimulus function is changed—if, in other terms, the individual's values change—the events in the environment would appear to be the same and to follow the individual's behavior just as they always did, but the individual's behavior would be under some different control. Thus, contingencies apparently the same would actually be different. Without detailed empirical analysis, however, it is not possible to know how intrusive the changes in stimulus function would have to be.

Why, then, do behavior analysts seek to eliminate crime by attending to individuals rather than to societal structures? An armchair analysis of the contingencies suggests several possible explanations. First, our present society supports programs that intervene on an individual level. Its support tends to be based on the conceptions that societal structures are not in need of change and that the causes of crime lie within the individual. The programs of the behavior analyst are supported because it is hoped that they will change the individual, that they will correct flawed and maladaptive personalities. Development of behavioral programs in prisons thus may involve the psychologist unintentionally in the support of conceptions inconsistent with the principles underlying behavior modification.

Perhaps there is another reason for intervening at an individual level: Psychologists want to bring about solutions to which they are a party, and they have the power to operate only on individuals, not on societal structures. Another possibility is that the societal changes that would be required to curb crime are so unappealing and aversive that psychologists engage in dealing with individuals because it is less aversive and more reinforcing.

As for what reinforces society for reinforcing psychologists for intervening on an individual level, this has been articulately stated in a speech to correctional psychologists by Judge David Bazelon (1973, p. 152): "In considering our motives for offering you a role, I think you would do well to consider how much less expensive it is to hire a thousand psychologists than to make even a miniscule change in the social and economic structure."

Summary and Conclusions

We have argued that the proper client of behavioral interventions—or any type of psychological interventions—in prisons is the prisoner, the one who is the subject of the intervention. At a minimum, the arguments presented in this part of the report provide a range of considerations that must be answered by those who would develop psychological programs in prisons. If the prisoner is taken as the proper agent with whom to negotiate regarding the means and goals of a program and if rehabilitation is a primary concern, we suggest that behavior analysts should conduct detailed empirical analyses of the societal contingencies that establish and maintain criminal behavior, as well as developing programs within prisons. Prison programs themselves should be negotiated with the prisoners and directed toward their release and successful integration into the appropriate community context. Whether such analyses of society will be done and such rehabilitation programs developed in addition to or even instead of the kind of prison program currently being conducted will depend on the prevailing contingencies influencing psychologists' behavior.

EIGHT

Society

In the cases that the commission investigated and that have been already reported, the psychologists designed interventions for individuals or small groups in special settings like the school, the prison cell block, or the community mental health center clinic. Behavior modification is also used by family members, to change the interactions within their family, and by individuals on themselves, to alter some aspect of their own behavior. In all these instances, the specific persons whose behavior is to be changed are identified (or at least identifiable) prior to the introduction of the intervention.

Increasingly, however, the techniques of behavior analysis are being directed toward change outside these limited settings. Behavior modification is coming to be used to deal with societal problems, and the interventions occur in open society. In such cases, the particular individuals who will become subject to the contingencies established by the intervention are not known until they actually contact those contingencies. The interventions are designed to alter the nature of the environment's reactions to individuals' behavior, whoever those individuals may be and whenever they come in contact with the redesigned environment.

Regrettably, the commission conducted no case study of this type of use of behavior technology. Thus we will touch only briefly here on the relevant issues.

Before raising the issues, a few examples of the use of behavioral technology and environmental redesign in open society may help to convey a sense of the sort of interventions that are involved. Studies have been reported in which behavioral technology was used to motivate people to use public transportation instead of their cars (Everett, 1976; Everett, Hayward, and Meyers, 1974): Anyone riding a special bus during the experimental period received tokens exchangeable for a variety of backup reinforcers. Research has also attempted to get people to conserve gas when they use their cars (Foxx, 1976) and to recycle paper (Witmer and Geller, 1976). The literature on the control of littering is growing rapidly (Burgess, Clark, and Hendee, 1971; Chapman and Risley, 1974; Powers, Osborne, and Anderson, 1973). These studies typically show that providing reinforcers for picking up litter results in increased amounts of trash turned in. Another area related to environmental concerns where research is beginning is in the conservation of electric power (Kohlenberg, Phillips, and Proctor, 1976) and fuel oil (Seaver and Patterson, 1976).

Although most persons agree that conservation of resources and protection and maintenance of the environment are worthwhile values, agreement is certainly not universal. Behavior modification methods have also been used for more controversial goals. For example, an especially ambitious program is attempting to encourage the limitation of family size as a part of population control, by building a sizable trust fund for families that cooperate by remaining small (Burgess, 1976). Potentially still more controversial is the extension of contingency management into the factory, with the proclaimed objective of improving profits by getting more work from the workers without increasing their wages ("New Tool," 1971).

Highly controversial uses of behavior modification include the token economy-inspired programs in what were called the Token Civic Action Programs, used as part of pacification in Vietnam (Walters, 1968), and the pilot research in Thailand in which psychologists suggested that the usefulness of food as a reinforcer in a behavior control plan could be enhanced by crop destruction (American Institutes for Research, 1976).

The social programs mentioned thus far in this section were each designed by a behavioral professional on the basis of behavioral principles. Other social programs used to control citizens' behavior have been developed by nonprofessionals, using their nontechnical understanding of how human behavior can be controlled. Many such programs, based implicitly rather than explicitly on behavioral principles, have been instituted in our society and apply now or have applied in the past to wide segments of society. Such behavior control systems provide a model of the way that more explicit behavorial programs might be implemented once a behavioral professional has done the initial design and evaluation research. A few such programs will be mentioned briefly here, as examples.

Currently, traffic laws, fines, income tax laws, the Selective Service program, licensing and regulation procedures, and the criminal code generally—all are more or less systematic behavior control techniques. When the draft was in effect, for example, the consequences of refusing to register or of refusing induction were a maximum of five years in jail and a $10,000 fine. To give another example, the income tax system is designed to provide greater payoff and less cost for certain kinds of family structures. Until 1969, married persons paid a great deal less income tax than single persons; the differential since then has decreased, but it is still sizable. The income tax rules allow more deductions the more children you are rearing, and they charge less tax when one spouse does not work outside the home than when both spouses bring in an income. These and other regulations of the Internal Revenue Service provide monetary reinforcement and societal sanction for some behaviors and not others.

The Selective Service system, as it existed from the Korean

War until late into the Vietnam War, used a far-reaching behavior control system, although, as far as we know, the system was not designed with behavioral principles specifically in mind. The contingencies of the system were, however, designed so that the desired distribution of manpower in various educational tracks and careers would result. The system was described in a Selective Service document as follows:

> While the best-known purpose of Selective Service is to procure manpower for the armed forces, a variety of related processes takes place outside delivery of manpower to the active armed forces. Many of these may be put under the heading of "channeling manpower." Many young men would not have pursued a higher education if there had not been a program of student deferment. Many young scientists, engineers, tool-and-die makers, and other possessors of scarce skills would not remain in their jobs in the defense effort if it were not for a program of occupational deferments. Even though the salary of a teacher has historically been meager, many young men remain in that job, seeking the reward of a deferment. The process of channeling manpower by deferment is entitled to much credit for the large number of graduate students in technical fields and for the fact that there is not a greater shortage of teachers, engineers and other scientists working in activities which are essential to the national interest [*Selective Service Orientation Kit,* 1965].

The avoidance contingencies used by the Selective Service were described by the service as the "club of induction" (*Selective Service Orientation Kit,* 1965). Other procedures of the Selective Service also used the highly aversive consequence of induction to shape desired behavior. For example, older males were drafted first, rather than eighteen-year-olds, so that younger males would be subjected for the longest possible period to the threat of induction (*Selective Service Orientation Kit,* 1965). Similarly, physical examinations were given late because "Once the label of 'rejectee' is upon him, all efforts at guidance by persuasion are futile. If he attempts to enlist at seventeen or eighteen and is rejected, then he receives virtually none of the impulsion the system is capable of giving him. If he makes no effort to enlist and as a result is not rejected until delivered for examination by the Selective Service system at about age twenty-three, he has felt some of the pressure but thereafter is a free agent" (*Selective Service Orientation Kit,* 1965).

Identification of the Client

When behavioral professionals engage in change at the societal level, when interventions affect whole classes of persons, perhaps in large geographic areas, the psychologists are typically employed by the municipality or state. Interventions in industry are planned by psychologists working for the corporation involved. Exceptions occur when such intervention programs are part of psychologists' research; the professionals then would be in the employ of a university. In all these cases, however, the persons directly affected by the new technology are not the psychologists' employers, and typically they have no opportunity to negotiate goals or means with the psychologists. For example, unless a union contract specifies it, workers in industries do not have the right to consent (or object) to proposed changes in management practices. Rather, in most corporations, management selects the goals, such as particular products or profit margins.

Psychologists should be sensitive to the implications of their dual allegiance both to the economic interests of their employers and to the persons affected by their programs. Psychologists are hired by institutions, industries, municipalities, and states to help those organizations meet their objectives; continued employment, raises, and promotions are the reinforcers used to control the psychologists' behavior. The threat of losing those reinforcers makes the probability low of countering the organizations' objectives, unless the psychologists are willing to find another position.

An alternative is for psychologists to make their talents and skills available to organizations that represent the disadvantaged, to civil liberties groups, and to organizations that seek to diminish sexism, racism, and ageism. Behavioral psychologists could analyze the controlling contingencies in society's traditional management systems, develop effective countercontrol techniques, and communicate these to people who otherwise lack sufficient power to confront the system. The psychologists would thus be working for the persons affected, rather than for the controlling organizations.

Selection of Goals

Large-scale implementation of behavioral technology is still a prospect for the future, as far as most of the programs designed by behavior analysts are concerned. However, in reality there seems to be little reason to expect that citizens' roles in setting goals for such programs will be different from what has happened with other programs currently in effect and designed by nonpsychologists. At the most, the citizens' input has been through the electoral process. This gives the citizens participation in goal setting in a much more general way and in a quite different sense than is usually involved in the psychologist-client relationship.

The main recourse of persons subjected unwillingly to behavior technology is likely to be the same as their recourse whenever unpopular social programs are instituted: noncompliance. Noncompliance of large numbers of people with population policy goals and birth control technology is a major problem in many countries of the world; systematic noncompliance with tax laws is also said to be a serious problem in countries other than the United States; noncompliance with the draft and rebellion by those in military service became an issue in the United States during the Vietnam War; and noncompliance with court-ordered busing to end segregation is a continuing problem in the United States.

Protection of the Clients' Rights

A major issue when behavioral interventions are conducted in society at large is whether the persons subjected to the intervention can be said, in any sense, to have consented to participate.

In some cases, consent was obtained from individual participants in the pilot stage, but obtaining consent when the program is implemented on a larger scale would be impossible. In the household energy conservation plan, for example, the subjects who participated in the pilot testing volunteered, much like subjects for typical laboratory experiments, and were offered a modest inducement of small financial gain. Once the program is developed, it could presumably be implemented on a community, state, or even national basis. In the area where it is implemented, voluntary participation is unlikely to be sought. It is also questionable whether the psychologists who designed the program originally would have a meaningful input or supervisory role at this later stage.

In some cases, individual consent is not obtained in a formal way even for participation in the pilot studies, but an informal type of consent does occur. In the studies of bus riding, for example, only some of the buses on the route were experimental buses; individuals could ride buses that dispensed tokens, or they could ride other buses. Again, once such a program is shown to be successful, all available buses are likely to be involved.

Sometimes the intervention is undertaken in such a way that all the persons in the target environment must participate, because no meaningful options are available to them. Workers can refuse to participate in programs instituted in factories only by endangering their jobs; peasants cannot prevent defoliation of their crops by airborne chemicals.

Thus, to varying degrees, all programs conducted in an open society raise the issue of the adequacy of informed consent by those who participate. Because in most cases the purpose of pilot work is to develop environmental design technology that can be applied on a larger scale, virtually any instance of this type of behavior modification intervention will eventually be faced with the consent issue. The fully implemented behavior control system is no less an example of behavior modification for the lack of the continued presence of the psychologist who developed the technological application. The consent problem is particularly thorny because in virtually all these applications the particular individuals who will be subjected to the intervention cannot be identified until they have begun to contact the redesigned contingencies.

Society already engages in a wide variety of behavior control techniques, of course. These societal controls have citizens' consent in that each of us subscribes to the social contract, and our continued presence in our society implies that we consent to any social control programs that are instituted. Failing to consent constitutes civil disobedience, and those who refuse to participate may be subject to legally prescribed sanctions.

Ideally, when a new social control program is contemplated, citizens who will be affected by it should have the opportunity to evaluate its goals, methods, and ethics, either directly or through their elected representatives. In this evaluation, the new technology and its potential benefits should be considered in relation to current societal practices and values and to the costs and benefits of existing technology.

The Role of the Psychologist in Institutional Change

Psychologists can take several different positions with regard to stability and change in our society. They can use their knowledge about human behavior to alter the environment so as to have people behave the way those in power—those with control over reinforcers—wish and will reinforce. They can also design programs to change people's behavior to fit them into existing environments. As noted earlier, in the chapters on prisons, some of the opposition to behavior modification derives from concern that psychologists have used the techniques of behavior modification to adjust powerless people to intolerable environments created by those in power. Alternatively, psychologists may be able to change the environment so markedly that the result is a change in society, rather than a change in an individual client's behavior.

Psychologists' behavior, like their clients', is controlled by consequences, including consequences from society, from their peers, and from their clients. Most behavior therapists, receiving their reinforcers from their employers and from peers who have similar reinforcements histories, define their clients' problems as existing within the clients, as a result of their reinforcement histories. The goal of treatment, then, is to change the clients' behavior. For example, rebellious schoolchildren are taught to follow rules, and alcoholic persons are punished for drinking or trained to make social responses considered more adaptive.

Other professionals' reinforcers appear to come from a subset of society that favors institutional change and from clients otherwise lacking in power. For these psychologists, actions designed to produce social and institutional change are likely to be high-probability behaviors. These may range from teaching and public information campaigns designed to inform people about the principles of behavior and about how contingencies can be used to control behavior, to active participation in social movements whose goal is to modify society's contingencies.

Psychologists who favor institutional change see individuals' behavior as a result of larger societal forces, and they focus their interventions on society, rather than on the individual. In their view, because behavior is considered to be constantly adjusting to prevailing contingencies in the environment, troublesome behavior calls for an analysis and change of the troublesome circumstances producing the behavior. For example, if schoolchildren are rebellious, these behavior analysts might examine the classroom activities to see if they are boring or aversive and to determine how they might be changed. The problem of alcoholism might be dealt with by raising questions about the many pressures for the consumption of alcohol, such as cocktail parties, attractive advertising, and interpersonal activities for which drinking alcohol is an essential entrance behavior (Holland, in press).

Behavior analysts who focus exclusively on social change criticize approaches to altering behavior labeled as deviant that favor change in the behavior of the individual emitting the deviant behavior. This point of view is very like that of the prisoner- and patient-advocacy groups, groups that often find behavior modification a prime target. Thus, although social action groups and behavioral professionals do not often cooperate, they seem to be natural allies, since both may advocate change in society's institutions.

Summary and Conclusions

Behavior analysts consider their role to be the analysis of the contingencies that create and maintain behavior. To the extent that the contingencies producing deviant behavior reflect the usual interactions between people and some organization or aspect of society, the behavior analyst studies those contingencies and recommends changes in them that would result in more favorable contingencies and less deviant behavior. In practice, of course, the situation is much more complicated than this, and the focus of intervention cannot so readily be centered on the environment *versus* the individual.

NINE

Recommendations

One possible result of the commission's deliberations could have been to draw up some guidelines for the practice of behavior modification. People often call for such guidelines, and the commission considered some possible reasons why calls for guidelines have been made, as well as the advantages and disadvantages of having guidelines.*

Why People Feel There Should Be Guidelines

Earlier chapters have discussed the kinds of problems leading people to recommend the preparation of guidelines for the ethical practice of behavior modification. To mention a few of these, people are afraid of being controlled, they are increasingly concerned with

* Stolz (1977), a member of the commission, had presented this logic and these conclusions elsewhere.

how society deals with deviance, they are increasingly sensitive to the impact resulting from the therapist's having more power than the client, and they may well also be reacting to extravagant claims made by some behavior analysts.

Although behavior modification may be no more subject to these concerns or criticisms than other types of therapeutic interventions, behavior modification seems to have acted like a "lightning rod" (Brown, Wienckowski, and Stolz, 1975) in the midst of the current stormy ethical and legal controversies, drawing to it these highly charged issues. Many writers have indicated that their special concern about behavior modification arises because they feel it is relatively effective, as compared with other forms of intervention, or because they feel it can more easily be abused in institutional settings, compared to other interventions. Persons opposed to the use of behavior modification in institutions have pointed to its potential as a tool by which those in charge can manage and manipulate those in their care, and as a way of appearing to improve what otherwise might be seen as a defective institution in need of major reform. The explicit use of aversive control in behavior modification practice has also attracted much critical attention.

In addition, specific abuses have been attributed to behavior modification programs, either justly or unjustly. The use of Anectine to punish prisoners has been described as behavior modification (Reimringer, Morgan, and Bramwell, 1970), and time out, which is only effective when used in a setting where behavior is also positively reinforced and when used for short periods of time (that is, a few minutes), has, in some settings, involved extraordinarily long periods of isolation in small quarters—again described as behavior modification (Opton, 1974). On the other hand, the consultative committees of the Association for the Advancement of Behavior Therapy have investigated a few cases where apparently qualified behavioral professionals were in charge of behavior modification programs in which punishment contingencies were misapplied and clients' rights violated.

Thus, people have been concerned broadly about any systematic attempt to change behavior and particularly about behavior modification. Professionals engaging in all types of psychological intervention have until recently been remiss, especially in regard to the extent to which clients were involved in decisions about the means and goals of interventions. In making those decisions, behavioral professionals, like other intervention agents, have tended to use their status and its associated control of relevant reinforcers as the rationale for making decisions unilaterally, with little or no serious consultation with the clients. Further, some behavioral professionals, again together with other psychologists, have lacked sensitivity to the issues involved in the decision about which behaviors will be defined as deviant.

Guidelines That Have Been Suggested

Numerous agencies, organizations, associations, and states have suggested guidelines specifically for the practice of behavior modification. So many different guidelines have been suggested or adopted for the regulation of behavior modification that it would take far more space than is justified to describe them all here. They range from the somewhat specific to the highly specific, from guidelines reflecting a correct understanding of the manner in which behavioral interventions are applied to those that seem to have been developed in the absence of information about the practice of behavior modification.

Guidelines for behavior modification often

- Involve the establishment of extensive systems of committees to monitor the interventions
- Emphasize the involvement of the persons whose behavior is to be changed, their representatives, or their attorneys, as well as citizen representatives
- Detail extensive, explicit procedures for obtaining informed consent
- Involve potentially long delays between the planning of a new intervention and its implementation in practice
- Are based on current or forecasted legal rulings and scientific knowledge existing at the time the guidelines were formulated

- Prescribe or proscribe specific procedures in specific circumstances
- Describe in detail the qualifications of intervention personnel

Reasons Not to Have Guidelines for Behavior Modification

The commission takes the position that it would be unwise for the American Psychological Association to enunciate guidelines for the practice of behavior modification. The procedures of behavior modification appear to be no more or less subject to abuse and no more or less in need of ethical regulation than intervention procedures derived from any other set of principles and called by other terms.

The regulation of behavior modification could have unfortunate side effects as well. If only behavior modification and no other psychological intervention were to be regulated by guidelines, this regulation would be likely to lead to the demise of the practice of behavior modification in those settings to which the guidelines applied. If institutional staff can use any other intervention, an intervention that seems like behavior modification but is not so labeled, or no intervention at all, without going through the sets of review committees and special consent procedures required for behavioral interventions, Goldiamond (1975, 1976) has argued that they will use the administratively simpler procedures; that is, those that do not entail additional annoyance, delay, and cost.

Furthermore, specific prescriptive and proscriptive guidelines could have a stultifying or freezing effect on developments within the field (Agras, 1973). This is especially so when guidelines are legislatively enacted but may also be for administratively enacted guidelines. Law and science are constantly changing; guidelines drawing on the current legal and scientific situation may be rapidly outdated as new decisions are made and new data are forthcoming.

On the other hand, guidelines can be used to protect practices and institutions that are under attack; that is, they can serve a function opposite from that for which they were originally created. Procedures meeting the letter but not the spirit of a set of guidelines may be sheltered from criticism because of the guidelines.

Should the attempt be made to write a set of guidelines that would apply to all sorts of interventions? All psychological interventions, after all, confront the same ethical problems of goals and techniques as behavior modification does. The problem then arises that critical aspects of the intervention process vary so widely across settings and populations that it becomes virtually impossible to write something that can adequately cover all possibilities and yet be effective. Looked at in the broadest sense, society is replete with behavior-influencing techniques, including public education, advertising, the criminal justice system, and self-help and self-development programs. These techniques too share the ethical problems of interventions identified more directly with psychology and with behavior modification.

It is even difficult to construct guidelines suitable for regulating the use of behavior modification and other types of psychological interventions in the simplest of cases, that of a middle-class client who comes to a therapist for treatment on an out-patient basis for a problem defined by the client. Because the therapist and the client are similar in status and culture, they will tend to agree on values, and ethical conflicts will be minimal. Even so, issues can arise about the appropriateness of the client's goals for treatment.

Moreover, several authors have argued that clinicians using behavioral methods should seriously question whether the behavior they are being asked to change should in fact be changed (Begelman, 1975; Davison, 1976; O'Leary, 1972; Serber and Keith, 1974), generally on the grounds that the client's goals may be too far from the therapist's own values.

Truly adequate guidelines for interventions should deal with the much more complex issues that arise when the situation is more complicated than in the example of the middle-class adult out-patient. In earlier sections of this book, we described some of these complications in each of the settings we investigated. When the psychologist owes allegiance to someone other than the people whose behavior is to be changed; when those people are, for any reason, not clearly competent to make decisions about the means and goals of the intervention; when their ability to consent freely to the intervention can be questioned for any reason—then the problem of adequate guidelines becomes increasingly difficult to solve. Both lawyers and psychologists—including those who are members of the commission—differ sharply among themselves on these and other questions, making it difficult to arrive at a consensus about how the issues should be dealt with in a set of guidelines.

Stolz (in press, a) has suggested that offering individuals a choice of interventions, an appealing idea and one found in most sets of guidelines, is an illusory solution. If psychologists offer their clients a choice of interventions, the very alternatives they choose to present may be considered a reflection of the influences on the psychologists' behavior. For example, psychologists working for mental hospitals and prisons have, in the past, tended to select as potential goals for interventions those behaviors that are conducive to the maintenance of good order on the ward or cell block (Holland, 1975; Shaw, 1972). On the other hand, psychologists with other values might recommend interventions designed to foster social change. Behavior analysts whose interventions are part of their research programs will describe the alternatives in such a way that they can get enough subjects for their studies (Barber, Lally, Makaruska, and Sullivan, 1973; Beecher, 1966; Gray, 1975).

Providing advocates for the clients, or establishing an advisory committee, does not make the choice any less an illusory one, in Stolz's (in press, a) view, because the behavior of the advocate or the members of the committee is, like all other behavior, responsive to social contingencies. A method that may maximize the extent to which the contingencies on the behavior of all parties are made explicit is to have alternative interventions described by individuals who are advocates of those methods.

Alternatives to Guidelines

Serious problems face any attempt to develop guidelines for behavior modification. We do not mean to imply that behavior modification therefore should be left unmonitored. Rather, like other interventions, behavior modification falls under the general ethical principles to which all practitioners subscribe.

Recommendations

Thus, *our primary recommendation* is that persons engaged in any type of psychological intervention subscribe to and follow the ethics codes and standards of their professions. For psychologists, the current version of the ethics code is the American Psychological Association's *Ethical Standards of Psychologists: 1977 Revision* (1977a, reprinted at the end of this book). Other official policy statements of the APA that are relevant to psychological interventions include the *Standards for Providers of Psychological Services* (American Psychological Association, 1977b, reprinted at the end of this book), a statement on psychology as a profession (American Psychological Association, 1968), *Ethical Principles in the Conduct of Research with Human Participants* (American Psychological Association, 1973), and the *Standards for Educational and Psychological Tests* (American Psychological Association, 1974).

Each of these codes and standards includes provisions relevant to any type of psychological intervention, including behavior modification. For example, the *Ethical Standards of Psychologists: 1977 Revision* includes the following provisions:

> *Principle 1e.* As practitioners, psychologists know that they bear a heavy social responsibility because their recommendations and professional actions may alter the lives of others. They are alert to personal, social, organizational, financial, or political situations or pressures that might lead to misuse of their influence.
>
> *Principle 3c.* In providing psychological services, psychologists avoid any action that will violate or diminish the legal and civil rights of clients or of others who may be affected by their actions. . . .
>
> *Principle 6.* Psychologists respect the integrity and protect the welfare of the people and groups with whom they work. When there is conflict of interest between the client and the psychologist's employing institution, psychologists clarify the nature and direction of their loyalties and responsibilities and keep all parties informed of their commitments. Psychologists fully inform consumers as to the purpose and nature of an evaluative,

> treatment, educational, or training procedure, and they freely acknowledge that clients, students, or participants in research have freedom of choice with regard to participation.
>
> *Principle 6e.* The psychologist attempts to terminate a clinical or consulting relationship when it is reasonably clear that the consumer is not benefiting from it. Psychologists who find that their services are being used by employers in a way that is not beneficial to the participants, or to employees who may be affected, or to significant others have the responsibility to make their observations known to the responsible persons and to propose modification or termination of the engagement.

Each of the ethical standards just quoted relates to an issue discussed in our report; that is, the *Ethical Standards of Psychologists: 1977 Revision* contains material directly relevant to the practice of behavior modification.

Second, *we recommend* that the American Psychological Association consider adopting a brief checklist of issues that could be used in the evaluation of the ethics of any psychological intervention. This would be more detailed and specific than the APA *Ethical Standards of Psychologists* and would be more directly focused on issues relating to clients' rights than the APA *Standards for Providers of Psychological Services.* The checklist would raise ethical issues related to psychological interventions. As we have argued earlier, we do not feel it is appropriate for such a checklist to be adopted specifically for behavior modification. As a result, we hereby recommend the adoption of the checklist to the American Psychological Association as a whole.

The following checklist was developed on the basis of a consideration of the issues as we saw them raised in the case studies, and it stresses protection of the client's rights.* Ideally, before the checklist of issues is adopted by the American Psychological Association to apply to all psychological interventions, it should be evaluated in

* This checklist was developed with the assistance of a committee of the Association for Advancement of Behavior Therapy.

practice by a wide range of practitioners. Thus, as part of our second recommendation to the APA, we suggest that the task of monitoring such an evaluation be assigned to one of the standing boards.

A checklist of issues is, of course, subject to the criticisms already discussed with regard to the development of guidelines for behavior modification; it would even be possible to treat the following questions as if they were a set of guidelines, prescriptions, and proscriptions. However, the intent of the commission is that the checklist should function to raise issues, not to resolve them, and that consideration of the issues should focus attention on aspects of the therapeutic process that potentially put clients at risk. If the checklist is viewed within the context of the complexity of the issues involved and if the relevant risks and benefits are balanced, the resulting evaluation of interventions may result in increased attention to the clients' rights. It does not, of course, assure that interventions involve nothing illegal.

The following issues have been formulated to be relevant to any psychological intervention and to continue to be applicable even as legal and scientific standards change. The overall thrust of the issues reflects our decision to emphasize a basic respect for the client's right to participate voluntarily in psychological interventions; the client's rights are recognized at every stage of the intervention. (A comparable checklist of issues was developed independently by Martin, 1975.)

On each of the issues, ideal psychological interventions would have maximum involvement by the person whose behavior is to be changed, and the fullest possible consideration of societal pressures on that person, the psychologist, and the psychologist's employer. We recognize that the practicalities of actual settings sometimes require trade-offs among competing values and exceptions based on the exigencies of a particular case. For example, institutionalized mental patients may not be competent to make judgments about their own treatment, and either they may not have relatives or a guardian who can be contacted or the relatives or guardian may not have sufficient investment to assist the patient in making decisions regarding the planning of an intervention. Rather than recommending that such patients be prevented from participating in psychological interventions, we suggest that institutions consider protecting these patients' rights by having a broadly constituted review committee evaluate the appropriateness of proposed programs and monitor the programs after they are put into effect. As we have already noted, this is not a perfect solution; rather, it is a trade-off that attempts to deal with situations as they exist and to consider the potential benefit for the patient in the context of the risks entailed in a course of action.

In short, we feel there may be occasions when exceptions can be consistent with ethical practice; when exceptions are made, however, a demonstration is needed that the benefit to the clients will outweigh the risk to them from any diminution of their rights. Further, in some situations, the issues raised may not be relevant or may be reasonably modified in the light of local circumstances. We suggest, however, that it is essential for intervention programs to consider each of these issues, even though something less than ideal practice may eventually be adopted.

In the following checklist, the term *client* is used to describe the person whose behavior is to be changed; *intervention* and *problem behavior,* although used in the singular, refer to any and all interventions and problems being evaluated with the checklist. Initially, issues relevant to all settings are listed; these need to be qualified with the additional questions that follow, when someone other than the person whose behavior is to be changed is paying the psychologist or when that person's competence or the voluntary nature of that person's consent is questioned.

Checklist of Ethical Issues

Issues Relevant to All Settings

- *Selection of goals.* Before selecting the goals of the intervention, has the client explained to the psychologist what the client sees as the problem behavior? Has the psychologist determined and explained to the client, as well as possible, what might be causing the problem behavior? Have the psychologist and the client together chosen the goals of the intervention? Are the goals realistic, explicit, and positive? In the client's opinion, do they primarily serve the client's interests? Have alternative goals and their implications been explored? Are goals regularly reviewed? Whenever goals are changed, is it again done by mutual agreement between psychologist and client?

- *Selection of the intervention method.* Prior to the start of the intervention, has the psychologist explained to the client, in a way that the client can understand, the alternative methods that might be used to achieve these goals? If the proposed intervention is unpleasant, seriously intrusive, or irreversible, has consultation with persons advocating alternative approaches been made available? Have the psychologist and client together chosen the intervention methods from among the alternatives available? Are these methods consistent with current legal rulings and the APA ethical standards? Have the psychologist and client reviewed the evidence for the efficacy of the methods under consideration? Have they also reviewed the evidence for side effects of those methods, both positive and negative? Whenever the methods are changed, is it again done by mutual agreement between psychologist and client?
- *Type of intervention.* Are the intervention methods selected the least coercive, least punitive, and least intrusive methods currently available relative to the benefits expected?
- *Accountability.* Have the effects of the intervention been monitored before, during, and after its termination? Has progress been systematically evaluated? Is the intervention modified as necessary in response to this evaluation? Have the results been shared with the client?
- *Generalization.* Are there explicit and realistic plans for the transition to the postintervention period? Have these plans been developed together with the client, and have the client and anyone else involved agreed to cooperate?
- *Competence of psychologist or other individual conducting the intervention.* Is the person qualified to offer the intervention, or has appropriate supervision been arranged for? Has the client been informed about the qualifications of the intervention agent?

- *Confidentiality.* Has confidentiality of information been appropriately maintained? Does the client know what records are being kept and for what purpose? Is access to these records controlled by the client?
- *Right to terminate an intervention.* Has the client been told that, at all times during the intervention program, the intervention can be refused or terminated without prejudice of any kind? Does the client understand that this right is available and know how to exercise it?
- *Outside review.* Are the interventions used and goals chosen open to the scrutiny of the psychologist's peers and also to public scrutiny? Has a mechanism been established to enable peer review and public scrutiny?

Additional Issues Relevant When the Psychologist Has Dual Allegiance

In some settings, the psychologist is responsible both to the person whose behavior is to be changed by the intervention and to some other individual or organization that has hired the psychologist. The psychologist then may have special problems resulting from this dual allegiance. All the issues raised in the preceding section apply. In addition, the following issues are pertinent:

- *Selection of goals.* As part of the goal selection process, has the psychologist explained to the client the goals of the individual or organization hiring the psychologist? Has the client agreed to these goals?
- *Appropriateness of goals.* Have the psychologist and the client or the client's representative considered whether the goals selected are appropriate for this person? Are the goals realistic, explicit, and positive? Has the intervention been designed so the client is the one primarily benefiting from it?
- *Consideration of the client's rights.* Have the issues relevant to all settings been raised with an advisory committee that includes the psychologist conducting the intervention, other psychologists, the client or the client's advocate, guardian, or elected

representative, and a representative of the individual or organization that has hired the psychologist?

- *Community involvement.* Do persons in the community, other than those directly involved with the intervention, have an opportunity to evaluate whether the program offers adequate protection for the client's rights? Are these persons independent of the individual or organization that hired the psychologist? Has a mechanism been established to enable community involvement?

Additional Issues Relevant When the Client's Competence Is Questioned

- *Assessment of competence.* Has the client's competence to make decisions about the intervention been assessed recently and as objectively as possible?
- *Attempt to communicate.* Has the psychologist attempted to describe the goals and methods of the intervention in a sufficiently simple way that the client might be able to understand? Has the client's understanding of the goals and methods been assessed objectively?
- *Consideration of the client's rights.* Have the issues relevant to all settings been raised with the person legally responsible for the client?
- *Community involvement.* Do persons from the community, other than those directly involved in the intervention, have an opportunity to evaluate whether the intervention offers appropriate protection for the client's rights? Are these persons independent of the individual or organization that hired the psychologist? Has a mechanism been established to enable community involvement?

Additional Issues Relevant When the Voluntary Nature of the Client's Consent Is Questioned

- *Consideration of the client's rights.* Have the issues relevant to all settings been raised with an advisory committee that includes the client's representatives and members of the community, including persons with appropriate legal backgrounds?

- *Nonstandard interventions.* When the efficacy of the intervention is not well established, have special precautions been taken to avoid coercion or special inducements?
- *Right to terminate the intervention.* Have special efforts been made to ensure that the client understands that refusal to cooperate with the intervention will not result in the client's losing existing privileges or receiving additional punishment?

Summary and Conclusions

The commission's analysis of the advantages and disadvantages of having guidelines for the practice of behavior modification resulted in our not recommending the adoption of prescriptive and proscriptive guidelines. Rather, we recommend (1) that persons engaged in any type of psychological intervention subscribe to and follow the ethics codes and standards of their professions and (2) that the American Psychological Association consider adopting a brief checklist of issues that could be used in the evaluation of the ethics of any psychological intervention. In addition, we suggest that the checklist be evaluated in practice and that the task of monitoring the evaluation be assigned to one of the APA's standing boards.

Our report has not attempted to describe the procedures of behavior modification, to analyze the efficacy of behavioral interventions, or to compare the efficacy of behavior modification with that of other psychological interventions. Rather, we have described the major ethical problems that arise in connection with psychological interventions.

Although behavior modification may appear to present special or unique ethical issues, our analysis suggests that all psychological interventions share similar ethical problems and raise comparable ethical issues. It is our hope that the checklist of issues we have developed for the evaluation of psychological interventions will result in greater concern for these important issues and increased protection for clients' rights.

Ethical Standards of Psychologists: 1977 Revision

American Psychological Association

Climaxing nine years of work by several task forces and the Committee on Scientific and Professional Ethics and Conduct (CSPEC), draft 11 of the Ethical Standards of Psychologists went to the Council of Representatives at its January 28–30, 1977 meeting. A number of changes were made in the document by the council, resulting in draft 12, which was adopted on January 30th, in the form printed as follows.

Because the council could not agree on several sections of Principle 5 (Confidentiality), the final action was to approve the final revised draft with the exception of this principle. The old principle (formerly Principle 6 in the Ethical Standards as printed in the 1975 Biographical Directory) will hold until a revision has been adopted by the council.

Council comments and suggestions applicable to this section are now being solicited by CSPEC. The council also directed the committee to take into account the forthcoming report of the Task Force on Privacy and Confidentiality, as well as upcoming federal regulations covering similar matters. APA members having specific wording changes to suggest may send them to Brenda Gurel, Secretary, CSPEC, APA, 1200 Seventeenth Street, N.W., Washington, D.C. 20036.

Preamble

Psychologists[1,2] respect the dignity and worth of the individual and honor the preservation and protection of fundamental human rights. They are committed to increasing knowledge of human behavior and of people's understanding of themselves and others and to the utilization of such knowledge for the promotion of human welfare. While pursuing these endeavors, they make every effort to protect the welfare of those who seek their services or of any human being or animal that may be the object of study. They use their skills only for purposes consistent with these values and do not knowingly permit their misuse by others. While demanding for themselves freedom of inquiry and communication, psychologists accept the responsibility this freedom requires: competence, objectivity in the application of skills, and concern for the best interests of clients, colleagues, and society in general. In the pursuit of these ideals, psychologists subscribe to principles in the following areas: (1) responsibility, (2) competence, (3) moral and legal standards, (4) public statements, (5) confidentiality, (6) welfare of the consumer, (7) professional relationships, (8) utilization of assessment techniques, and (9) pursuit of research activities.

Principle 1. Responsibility

In their commitment to the understanding of human behavior, psychologists value objectivity and integrity, and in providing services they maintain the highest standards of their profession. They accept responsibility for the consequences of their work and make every effort to ensure that their services are used appropriately.

a. As scientists, psychologists accept the ultimate responsibility for selecting appropriate areas and methods most relevant to these areas. They plan their research in ways to minimize the possibility that their findings will be misleading. They provide thorough discussion of the limitations of their data and alternative hypotheses, especially where their work touches on social policy or might be construed to the detriment of persons in specific age, sex, ethnic, socioeconomic or other social groups. In publishing reports of their work, they never suppress disconfirming data. Psychologists take credit only for the work they have actually done.

   Psychologists clarify in advance with all appropriate persons or agencies the expectations for sharing and utilizing research data. They avoid dual relationships that may limit objectivity, whether political or monetary, so that interference with data, human participants, and milieu is kept to a minimum.

b. As employees of an institution or agency, psychologists have the responsibility of remaining alert to and attempting to moderate institutional pressures that may distort reports of psychological findings or impede their proper use.

c. As members of governmental or other organizational bodies, psychologists remain accountable as individuals to the highest standards of their profession.

d. As teachers, psychologists recognize their primary obligation to help others acquire knowledge and skill. They maintain high standards of scholarship and objectivity by presenting psychological information fully and accurately.

e. As practitioners, psychologists know that they bear a heavy social responsibility because their recommendations and professional actions may alter the lives of others. They are alert to personal, social, organizational, financial, or political situations or pressures that might lead to misuse of their influence.

f. Psychologists provide adequate and timely evaluations to employees, trainees, students, and others whose work they supervise.

Principle 2. Competence

The maintenance of high standards of professional competence is a responsibility shared by all psychologists in the interest of the public and the profession as a whole. Psychologists recognize the boundaries of their competence and the limitations of their techniques and only provide services, use techniques, or offer opinions as professionals that meet recognized standards. Psychologists maintain knowledge of current scientific and professional information related to the services they render.

a. Psychologists accurately represent their competence, education, training, and experience. Psychologists claim as evidence of professional qualifications only those degrees obtained from institutions acceptable under the bylaws and rules of council of the American Psychological Association.
b. As teachers, psychologists perform their duties on the basis of careful preparation so that their instruction is accurate, current, and scholarly.
c. Psychologists recognize the need for continuing education and are open to new procedures and changes in expectations and values over time. They recognize differences among people, such as those that may be associated with age, sex, socioeconomic, and ethnic backgrounds. Where relevant, they obtain training, experience, or counsel to assure competent service or research relating to such persons.
d. Psychologists with the responsibility for decisions involving individuals or policies based on test results have an understanding of psychological or educational measurement, validation problems, and other test research.
e. Psychologists recognize that their effectiveness depends in part on their ability to maintain effective interpersonal relations and that aberrations on their part may interfere with their abilities. They refrain from undertaking any activity in which their personal problems are likely to lead to inadequate professional services or harm to a client; or, if engaged in such activity when they become aware of their personal problems, they seek competent pro-

fessional assistance to determine whether they should suspend, terminate, or limit the scope of their professional and/or scientific activities.

Principle 3. Moral and Legal Standards

Psychologists' moral, ethical, and legal standards of behavior are a personal matter to the same degree as they are for any other citizen, except as these may compromise the fulfillment of their professional responsibilities or reduce the trust in psychology or psychologists held by the general public. Regarding their own behavior, psychologists should be aware of the prevailing community standards and of the possible impact on the quality of professional services provided by their conformity to or deviation from these standards. Psychologists are also aware of the possible impact of their public behavior on the ability of colleagues to perform their professional duties.

a. Psychologists as teachers are aware of the diverse backgrounds of students and, when dealing with topics that may give offense, treat the material objectively and present it in a manner for which the student is prepared.
b. As employees, psychologists refuse to participate in practices inconsistent with legal, moral, and ethical standards regarding the treatment of employees or of the public. For example, psychologists will not condone practices that are inhumane or that result in illegal or otherwise unjustifiable discrimination on the basis of race, age, sex, religion, or natural origin in hiring, promotion, or training.
c. In providing psychological services, psychologists avoid any action that will violate or diminish the legal and civil rights of clients or of others who may be affected by their actions.

   As practitioners, psychologists remain abreast of relevant federal, state, local, and agency regulations and Association standards of practice concerning the conduct of their practice. They are concerned with developing such legal and quasilegal regulations as best serve the public interest and in changing such existing regulations as are not beneficial to the interests of the public and the profession.

d. As researchers, psychologists remain abreast of relevant federal and state regulations concerning the conduct of research with human participants or animals.

Principle 4. Public Statements

Public statements, announcements of services, and promotional activities of psychologists serve the purpose of providing sufficient information to aid the consumer public in making informed judgments and choices. Psychologists represent accurately and objectively their professional qualifications, affiliations, and functions, as well as those of the institutions or organizations with which they or the statements may be associated. In public statements providing psychological information or professional opinions or providing information about the availability of psychological products and services, psychologists take full account of the limits and uncertainties of present psychological knowledge and techniques.

a. When announcing professional services, psychologists limit the information to name, highest relevant academic degree conferred, date and type of certification or licensure, diplomate status, address, telephone number, office hours, and, at the individual practitioner's discretion, an appropriate brief listing of the types of psychological services offered, and fee information. Such statements are descriptive of services provided but not evaluative as to their quality or uniqueness. They do not contain testimonials by quotation or by implication. They do not claim uniqueness of skills or methods unless determined by acceptable and public scientific evidence.
b. In announcing the availability of psychological services or products, psychologists do not display any affiliations with an organization in a manner that falsely implies the sponsorship or certification of that organization. In particular and for example,

psychologists do not offer APA membership or fellowship as evidence of qualification. They do not name their employer or professional associations unless the services are in fact to be provided by or under the responsible, direct supervision and continuing control of such organizations or agencies.

c. Announcements of "personal growth groups" give a clear statement of purpose and the nature of the experiences to be provided. The education, training, and experience of the psychologists are appropriately specified.

d. Psychologists associated with the development or promotion of psychological devices, books, or other products offered for commercial sale make every effort to ensure that announcements and advertisements are presented in a professional, scientifically acceptable, and factually informative manner.

e. Psychologists do not participate for personal gain in commercial announcements recommending to the general public the purchase or use of any proprietary or single-source product or service.

f. Psychologists who interpret the science of psychology or the services of psychologists to the general public accept the obligation to present the material fairly and accurately, avoiding misrepresentation through sensationalism, exaggeration, or superficiality. Psychologists are guided by the primary obligation to aid the public in forming their own informed judgments, opinions, and choices.

g. As teachers, psychologists ensure that statements in catalogues and course outlines are accurate and sufficient, particularly in terms of subject matter to be covered, bases for evaluating progress, and nature of course experiences. Announcements or brochures describing workshops, seminars, or other educational programs accurately represent intended audience and eligibility requirements, educational objectives, and nature of the material to be covered, as well as the education, training, and experience of the psychologists presenting the programs and any fees involved. Public announcements soliciting subjects for research and in which clinical services or other professional services are offered as an inducement make clear the nature of the services as well as the costs and other obligations to be accepted by the human participants of the research.

h. Psychologists accept the obligation to correct others who may represent the psychologist's professional qualifications or associations with products or services in a manner incompatible with these guidelines.
i. Psychological services for the purpose of diagnosis, treatment, or personal advice are provided only in the context of a professional relationship and are not given by means of public lectures or demonstrations, newspapers or magazine articles, radio or television programs, mail, or similar media.

Principle 5. Confidentiality

Safeguarding information about an individual that has been obtained by the psychologist in the course of his or her teaching, practice, or investigation is a primary obligation of the psychologist. Such information is not communicated to others unless certain important conditions are met.

a. Information received in confidence is revealed only after most careful deliberation and when there is clear and imminent danger to an individual or to society and then only to appropriate professional workers or public authorities.
b. Information obtained in clinical or consulting relationships, or evaluative data concerning children, students, employees, and others are discussed only for professional purposes and only with persons clearly concerned with the case. Written and oral reports should present only data germane to the purposes of the evaluation, and every effort should be made to avoid undue invasion of privacy.
c. Clinical and other materials are used in classroom teaching and writing only when the identity of the persons involved is adequately disguised.
d. The confidentiality of professional communications about individuals is maintained. Only when the originator and other persons

involved give their express permission is a confidential professional communication shown to the individual concerned. The psychologist is responsible for informing the client of the limits of the confidentiality.

e. Only after explicit permission has been granted is the identity of research subjects published. When data have been published without permission for identification, the psychologist assumes responsibility for adequately disguising their sources.
f. The psychologist makes provisions for the maintenance of confidentiality in the prevention and ultimate disposition of confidential records.

Principle 6. Welfare of the Consumer

Psychologists respect the integrity and protect the welfare of the people and groups with whom they work. When there is a conflict of interest between the client and the psychologist's employing institution, psychologists clarify the nature and direction of their loyalties and responsibilities and keep all parties informed of their commitments. Psychologists fully inform consumers as to the purpose and nature of an evaluative, treatment, educational, or training procedure, and they freely acknowledge that clients, students, or participants in research have freedom of choice with regard to participation.

a. Psychologists are continually cognizant of their own needs and of their inherently powerful position *vis à vis* clients, in order to avoid exploiting their trust and dependency. Psychologists make every effort to avoid dual relationships with clients and/or relationships that might impair their professional judgment or increase the risk of client exploitation. Examples of such dual relationships include treating employees, supervisees, close friends, or relatives. Sexual intimacies with clients are unethical.
b. Where demands of an organization on psychologists go beyond reasonable conditions of employment, psychologists recognize possible conflicts of interest that may arise. When such conflicts

occur, psychologists clarify the nature of the conflict and inform all parties of the nature and direction of the loyalties and responsibilities involved.

c. When acting as a supervisor, trainer, researcher, or employer, psychologists accord informed choice, confidentiality, due process, and protection from physical and mental harm to their subordinates in such relationships.

d. Financial arrangements in professional practice are in accord with professional standards that safeguard the best interests of the client and that are clearly understood by the client in advance of billing. Psychologists are responsible for assisting clients in finding needed services in those instances where payment of the usual fee would be a hardship. No commission, rebate, or other form of remuneration may be given or received for referral of clients for professional services, whether by an individual or by an agency. Psychologists willingly contribute a portion of their services to work for which they receive little or no financial return.

e. The psychologist attempts to terminate a clinical or consulting relationship when it is reasonably clear that the consumer is not benefiting from it. Psychologists who find that their services are being used by employers in a way that is not beneficial to the participants, to employees who might be affected, or to significant others have the responsibility to make their observations known to the responsible persons and to propose modification or termination of the engagement.

Principle 7. Professional Relationships

Psychologists act with due regard for the needs, special competencies, and obligations of their colleagues in psychology and other professions. Psychologists respect the prerogatives and obligations of the institutions or organizations with which they are associated.

a. Psychologists understand the areas of competence of related professions and make full use of all the professional, technical, and administrative resources that best serve the interests of consumers. The absence of formal relationships with other professional workers does not relieve psychologists of the responsibility of securing for their clients the best possible professional service, nor does it relieve them from the exercise of foresight, diligence, and tact in obtaining the complementary or alternative assistance needed by clients.

b. Psychologists know and take into account the traditions and practices of other professional groups with which they work and cooperate fully with members of such groups. If a consumer is receiving services from another professional, psychologists do not offer their services directly to the consumer without first informing the professional person already involved so that the risk of confusion and conflict for the consumer can be avoided.

c. Psychologists who employ or supervise other professionals or professionals in training accept the obligation to facilitate their further professional development by providing suitable working conditions, consultation, and experience opportunities.

d. As employees of organizations providing psychological services or as independent psychologists serving clients in an organizational context, psychologists seek to support the integrity, reputation, and proprietary rights of the host organization. When it is judged necessary in a client's interest to question the organization's programs or policies, psychologists attempt to effect change by constructive action within the organization before disclosing confidential information acquired in their professional roles.

e. In the pursuit of research, psychologists give sponsoring agencies, host institutions, and publication channels the same respect and opportunity for giving informed consent that they accord to individual research participants. They are aware of their obligation to future research workers and ensure that host institutions are given adequate information about the research and proper acknowledgement of their contributions.

f. Publication credit is assigned to all those who have contributed to a publication in proportion to their contribution. Major contributions of a professional character made by several persons to a common project are recognized by joint authorship, with the experimenter or author who made the principal contribution identified and listed first. Minor contributions of a professional character, extensive clerical or similar nonprofessional assistance, and other minor contributions are acknowledged in footnotes or in an introductory statement. Acknowledgment through specific citations is made for unpublished as well as published material that has directly influenced the research or writing. A psychologist who compiles and edits material of others for publication publishes the material in the name of the originating group, if any, and with his or her own name appearing as chairperson or editor. All contributors are to be acknowledged and named.

g. When a psychologist violates ethical standards, psychologists who know firsthand of such activities should, if possible, attempt to rectify the situation. Failing an informal solution, psychologists bring such unethical activities to the attention of the appropriate local, state, and/or national committee on professional ethics, standards, and practices.

h. Members of the Association cooperate with duly constituted committees of the Association—in particular and for example, the Committee on Scientific and Professional Ethics and Conduct and the Committee on Professional Standards Review—by responding to inquiries promptly and completely. Members taking longer than thirty days to respond to such inquiries shall have the burden of demonstrating that they acted with "reasonable promptness." Members also have a similar responsibility to respond with reasonable promptness to inquiries from duly constituted state association ethics committees and professional standards review committees.

Principle 8. Utilization of Assessment Techniques

In the development, publication, and utilization of psychological assessment techniques, psychologists observe relevant APA standards. Persons examined have the right to know the results, the interpretations made, and, where appropriate, the original data on which final judgments were based. Test users avoid imparting unnecessary information that would compromise test security, but they provide requested information that explains the basis for decisions that may adversely affect that person or that person's dependents.

a. The client has the right to have and the psychologist has the responsibility to provide explanations of the nature and the purposes of the test and the test results in language that the client can understand, unless, as in some employment or school settings, there is an explicit exception to this right agreed on in advance. When the explanations are to be provided by others, the psychologist establishes procedures for providing adequate explanations.
b. When a test is published or otherwise made available for operational use, it is accompanied by a manual (or other published or readily available information) that fully describes the development of the test, the rationale, and evidence of validity and reliability. The test manual explicitly states the purposes and applications for which the test is recommended and identifies special qualifications required to administer the test and to interpret it properly. Test manuals provide complete information regarding the characteristics of the normative population.
c. In reporting test results, psychologists indicate any reservations regarding validity or reliability resulting from testing circumstances or inappropriateness of the test norms for the person tested. Psychologists strive to ensure that the test results and their interpretations are not misused by others.
d. Psychologists accept responsibility for removing from clients' files test score information that has become obsolete, lest such information be misused or misconstrued to the disadvantage of the person tested.
e. Psychologists offering test scoring and interpretation services are able to demonstrate that the validity of the programs and procedures used in arriving at interpretations are based on appropriate evidence. The public offering of an automated test interpretation service is considered as a professional-to-professional consultation. The psychologist makes every effort to avoid misuse of test reports.

Ethical Issues in Behavior Modification

Principle 9. Pursuit of Research Activities

The decision to undertake research should rest on a considered judgment by the individual psychologist about how best to contribute to psychological science and to human welfare. Psychologists carry out their investigations with respect for the people who participate and with concern for their dignity and welfare.

a. In planning a study, the investigator has the responsibility for making a careful evaluation of its ethical acceptability, taking into account the following additional principles for research with human beings. To the extent that this appraisal, weighing scientific and humane values, suggests a compromise of any principle, the investigator incurs an increasingly serious obligation to seek ethical advice and to observe stringent safeguards to protect the rights of the human research participants.
b. Responsibility for the establishment and maintenance of acceptable ethical practice in research always remains with the individual investigator. The investigator is also responsible for the ethical treatment of research participants by collaborators, assistants, students, and employees—all of whom, however, incur parallel obligations.
c. Ethical practice requires the investigator to inform the participant of all features of the research that might reasonably be expected to influence willingness to participate and to explain all other aspects of the research about which the participant inquires. Failure to make full disclosure imposes additional force to the investigator's abiding responsibility to protect the welfare and dignity of the research participant.
d. Openness and honesty are essential characteristics of the relationship between investigator and research participant. When the methodological requirements of a study necessitate concealment or deception, the investigator is required to ensure as soon as possible the participant's understanding of the reasons for this action and of a sufficient justification for the procedures employed.
e. Ethical practice requires the investigator to respect the individ-

ual's freedom to decline to participate in or withdraw from research. The obligation to protect this freedom requires special vigilance when the investigator is in a position of power over the participant, as, for example, when the participant is a student, client, or employee or otherwise is in a dual relationship for the investigator.

f. Ethically acceptable research begins with the establishment of a clear and fair agreement between the investigator and the research participant that clarifies the responsibilities of each. The investigator has the obligation to honor all promises and commitments included in that agreement.

g. The ethical investigator protects participants from physical and mental discomfort, harm, and danger. If a risk of such consequences exists, the investigator is required to inform the participant of that fact, secure consent before proceeding and to take all possible measures to minimize distress. A research procedure must not be used if it is likely to cause serious or lasting harm to a participant.

h. After the data are collected, the investigator provides the participant with information about the nature of the study and to remove any misconceptions that may have arisen. Where scientific or human values justify delaying or withholding information, the investigator acquires a special responsibility to assure that there are no damaging consequences for the participant.

i. When research procedures may result in undesirable consequences for the individual participant, the investigator has the responsibility for detecting and removing or correcting these consequences, including, where relevant, long-term aftereffects.

j. Information obtained about the individual research participants during the course of an investigation is confidential unless otherwise agreed in advance. When the possibility exists that others may obtain access to such information, this possibility, together with the plans for protecting confidentiality, should be explained to the participants as part of the procedure for obtaining informed consent.

k. A psychologist using animals in research adheres to the provisions of the Rules Regarding Animals, drawn up by the Committee on Precautions and Standards in Animal Experimentation and adopted by the American Psychological Association.

l. Investigations of human participants using drugs should be conducted only in such settings as clinics, hospitals, or research facilities maintaining appropriate safeguards for the participants.

Notes

1. Approved by the Council of Representatives, January 30, 1977. Reprinted from the APA *Monitor,* March 1977.

2. A student of psychology who assumes the role of a psychologist shall be considered a psychologist for the purpose of this code of ethics.

References

Psychologists are responsible for knowing about and acting in accord with the standards and positions of the APA, as represented in such official documents as the following:

American Association of University Professors. "Statement on Principles on Academic Freedom and Tenure." *Policy Documents & Report,* 1977, 1–4.

American Psychological Association. *Guidelines for Psychologists for the Use of Drugs in Research.* Washington, D.C.: American Psychological Association, 1971.

American Psychological Association. *Principles for the Care and Use of Animals.* Washington, D.C.: American Psychological Association, 1971.

American Psychological Association. "Guidelines for Conditions of Employment of Psychologists." *American Psychologist,* 1972, *27,* 331–334.

American Psychological Association. "Guidelines for Psychologists Conducting Growth Groups." *American Psychologist,* 1973, *28,* 933.

American Psychological Association. *Ethical Principles in the Con-*

duct of Research with Human Participants. Washington, D.C.: American Psychological Association, 1973.

American Psychological Association. *Standards for Educational and Psychological Tests.* Washington, D.C.: American Psychological Association, 1974.

American Psychological Association. *Standards for Providers of Psychological Services.* Washington, D.C.: American Psychological Association, 1977.

Committee on Scientific and Professional Ethics and Conduct. "Guidelines for Telephone Directory Listings." *American Psychologist,* 1969, *24,* 70–71.

Standards for Providers of Psychological Services

American Psychological Association

In January 1975, the APA Council of Representatives created the original Committee on Standards for Providers of Psychological Services. The committee was charged with updating and revising the Standards adopted in September 1974. Members of the committee were Jacqueline C. Bouhoutsos, Leon Hall, Marian D. Hall, Mary Henle, Durand F. Jacobs (Chair), Abel Ossorio, and Wayne Sorenson. Task force liaison was Jerry H. Clark, and central office liaison was Arthur Centor.

In January 1976, the council further charged the committee to review the Standards and recommend revisions needed to reflect the varying needs of only those psychologists engaged in the activities of clinical, counseling, industrial-organizational, and school psychology. The committee was reconstituted with one member representing each of the four applied activities, plus one member representing institutional practice and one representing the public interest.

Members were Jules Barron, clinical; Barbara A. Kirk, counseling; Frank Friedlander, industrial-organizational (replacing Virginia Schein); Durand F. Jacobs (chair), institutional practice; M. Brewster Smith, public interest; Marian D. Hall, school; Arthur Centor was central office liaison.

The Standards that follow are the first revision of the national *Standards for Providers of Psychological Services* originally adopted by the American Psychological Association (APA) on September 4, 1974.[1] The intent of these Standards is to improve the quality, effectiveness, and accessibility of psychological services to all who require them.[2]

These Standards represent the attainment of a goal for which the Association has striven for over twenty years, namely, to codify a uniform set of standards for psychological practice that would serve the respective needs of users, providers, and third-party purchasers and sanctioners of psychological services. In addition, the Association has established a standing committee charged with keeping the Standards responsive to the needs of these groups and with upgrading and extending them progressively as the profession and science of psychology continue to develop new knowledge, improved methods, and additional modes of psychological service. These Standards have been established by organized psychology as a means of self-regulation to protect the public interest.

While these revised Standards contain a number of important changes, they differ from the original Standards in two major respects:

1. They uniformly specify the *minimally acceptable levels* of quality assurance and performance that providers of those psychological services covered by the Standards must reach or exceed. Care has

been taken to assure that each standard is clearly stated, readily measurable, realistic, and implementable.

2. The revised Standards apply to a more limited range of services than the original Standards. The present Standards have been restricted to applications in "human services" with the goal of facilitating more effective human functioning. The kinds of psychological services covered by the present Standards are those ordinarily involved in the practice of specialists in clinical, counseling, industrial-organizational, and school psychology. However, it is important to note that these Standards cover psychological functions and not classes of practitioners.

   Any persons representing themselves as psychologists, when providing any of the covered psychological service functions at any time and in any setting, whether public or private, profit or nonprofit, are required to observe these standards of practice in order to promote the best interests and welfare of the users of such services. It is to be understood that fulfillment of the requirements to meet these Standards shall be judged by peers in relation to the capabilities for evaluation and the circumstances that prevail in the setting at the time the program or service is evaluated.

Standards covering other psychological service functions may be added from time to time to those already listed. However, functions and activities related to the teaching of psychology, the writing or editing of scholarly or scientific manuscripts, and the conduct of scientific research do not fall within the purview of the present Standards.

Historical Background

Early in 1970, acting at the direction of the Association's Council of Representatives, the Board of Professional Affairs appointed a task force composed of practicing psychologists with specialized knowledge in at least one of every major class of human service facility and with experience relevant to the setting of standards. Its charge was to develop a set of standards for psychological practice. Soon thereafter, partial support for this activity was obtained through a grant from the National Institute of Mental Health.[3]

First, the task force established liaison with national groups already active in standard setting and accreditation. It was therefore able to influence the adoption of certain basic principles and wording contained in standards for psychological services published by the Joint Commission of Accreditation of Hospitals (JCAH) Accreditation Council for Facilities for the Mentally Retarded (1971) and by the Accreditation Council for Psychiatric Facilities (JCAH, 1972). It also contributed substantially to the "constitutionally required minimum standards for adequate treatment of the mentally ill" ordered by the U.S. District Court in Alabama (*Wyatt* v. *Stickney,* 1972). In concert with other APA committees, the task force also represented the Association in national-level deliberations with governmental groups and insurance carriers that defined the qualifications necessary for psychologists involved in providing health services.

These interim outcomes involved influence by the Association on actions by groups of nonpsychologists that directly affected the manner in which psychological services were employed, particularly in health and rehabilitation settings. However, these measures did not relieve the Association from exercising its responsibility for speaking out directly and authoritatively on what standards for psychological practice should be throughout a broad range of human service settings. It was also the responsibility of the Association to determine how psychologists would be held accountable should their practice fail to meet quality standards.

In September 1974, after more than four years of study and broad consultations, the task force proposed a set of standards, which the Association's Council of Representatives adopted and voted to publish in order to meet urgent needs of the public and the profession. Members of the council had various reservations about the scope and wording of the Standards as initially adopted. By establishing a continuing Committee on Standards, the council took the first step in what would be an ongoing process of review and revision.

The task of collecting, analyzing, and synthesizing reactions to the original Standards fell to two successive committees. They were charged similarly to review and revise the Standards and to suggest means to implement them, including their acceptance by relevant governmental and private accreditation groups. The dedicated work of the psychologists who served on both those committees is gratefully acknowledged. Also recognized with thanks are the several hundred comments received from scores of interested persons representing professional, academic, and scientific psychology, consumer groups, administrators of facilities, and others. This input from those directly affected by the original Standards provided the major stimulus and much of the content for the changes that appear in this revision.

Principles and Implications of the Standards

A few basic principles have guided the development of these Standards:

1. There should be a single set of standards that governs psychological service functions offered by psychologists, regardless of their specialty, setting, or form of remuneration. All psychologists in professional practice should be guided by a uniform set of standards, just as they are guided by a common code of ethics.
2. Standards should clearly establish minimally acceptable levels of quality for covered psychological service functions, regardless of the character of the users, purchasers, or sanctioners of such covered services.
3. All persons providing psychological services shall meet minimally acceptable levels of training and experience, which are consistent and appropriate with the functions they perform. However, final responsibility and accountability for services provided must rest with psychologists who have earned a doctoral degree in a program that is primarily psychological at a regionally accredited university or professional school. Those providing psychological services who have lesser (or other) levels of training shall be supervised by a psychologist with such training. This level of

qualification is necessary to assure that the public receives services of high quality.

4. There should be a uniform set of standards governing the quality of services to all users of psychological services in both the private and public sectors. There is no justification for maintaining the double standard presently embedded in most state legislation whereby providers of private fee-based psychological services are subject to statutory regulation, while those providing similar psychological services under governmental auspices are usually exempt from such regulations. This circumstance tends to afford greater protection under the law for those receiving privately delivered psychological services. On the other hand, those receiving privately delivered psychological services currently lack many of the safeguards that are available in governmental settings; these include peer review, consultation, record review, and staff supervision.
5. While assuring the user of the psychologist's accountability for the nature and quality of services rendered, standards must not constrain the psychologist from employing new methods or making flexible use of support personnel in staffing the delivery of services.

The Standards here presented have broad implications both for the public who use psychological services and for providers of such services:

1. Standards provide a firmer basis for a mutual understanding between provider and user and facilitate more effective evaluation of services provided and outcomes achieved.
2. Standards are an important step toward greater uniformity in legislative and regulatory actions involving providers of psychological services, and Standards provide the basis for the development of accreditation procedures for service facilities.
3. Standards give specific content to the profession's concept of ethical practice.
4. Standards have significant impact on tomorrow's training models for both professional and support personnel in psychology.

5. Standards for the provision of psychological services in human service facilities influence what is considered acceptable structure, budgeting, and staffing patterns in these facilities.
6. Standards are living documents that require continual review and revision.

The Standards illuminate weaknesses in the delivery of psychological services and point to their correction. Some settings are known to require additional and/or higher standards for specific areas of service delivery than those herein proposed. There is no intent to diminish the scope or quality of psychological services that exceed these Standards.

Systematically applied, these Standards serve to establish uniformly the minimally acceptable levels of psychological services. They serve to establish a more effective and consistent basis for evaluating the performance of individual service providers, and they serve to guide the organizing of psychological service units in human service settings.

Definitions

The term *providers of psychological services* refers to the following persons:

1. Professional psychologists.[4] Professional psychologists have a doctoral degree from a regionally accredited university or professional school in a program that is primarily psychological[5] and have appropriate training and experience in the area of service offered.[6]
2. All other persons who offer psychological services under the supervision of a professional psychologist.

The term *psychological services* refers to one or more of the following:[7]

1. Evaluation, diagnosis, and assessment of the functioning of individuals and groups in a variety of settings and activities.
2. Interventions to facilitate the functioning of individuals and

groups. Such interventions may include psychological counseling, psychotherapy, and process consultation.
3. Consultation relating to items 1 and 2.
4. Program development services in the areas of items 1, 2, and 3.[8]
5. Supervision of psychological services.

A *psychological service unit* is the functional unit through which psychological services are provided.

1. A psychological service unit is a unit that provides predominantly psychological services and is composed of one or more professional psychologists and supporting staff.
2. A psychological service unit may operate as a professional service or as a functional or geographic component of a larger governmental, educational, correction, health, training, industrial, or commercial organizational unit.[9]
3. A psychologist providing professional services in a multioccupational setting is regarded as a psychological service unit.
4. A psychological service unit also may be an individual or group of individuals in a private practice or a psychological consulting firm.

The term *user* includes

1. Direct users or recipients of psychological services.
2. Public and private institutions, facilities, or organizations receiving psychological services.
3. Third-party purchasers—those who pay for the delivery of services but who are not the recipients of services.

The term *sanctioners* refers to those users and nonusers who have a legitimate concern with the accessibility, timeliness, efficacy, and standards of quality attending the provision of psychological services. In addition to the users, sanctioners may include members of the user's family, the court, the probation officer, the school administrator, the employer, the union representative, the facility director, and so on. Another class of sanctioners is represented by various governmental, peer review, and accreditation bodies concerned with the assurance of quality.

Standard 1. Providers

1.1. Each psychological service unit offering psychological services shall have available at least one professional psychologist and as many more professional psychologists as are necessary to assure the quality of services offered.

Interpretation: The intent of this Standard is that one or more providers of psychological services in any psychological service unit shall meet the levels of training and experience of the professional psychologist as specified in the preceding definitions.[10]

When a professional psychologist is not available on a full-time basis, the facility shall retain the services of one or more professional psychologists on a regular part-time basis to supervise the psychological services provided. The psychologist(s) so retained shall have authority and participate sufficiently to enable him or her to assess the needs for services, review the content of services provided, and assume professional responsibility and accountability for them.

1.2. Providers of psychological services who do not meet the requirements for the professional psychologist shall be supervised by a professional psychologist who shall assume professional responsibility and accountability for the services provided. The level and extent of supervision may vary from task to task so long as the supervising psychologist retains a sufficiently close supervisory relationship to meet this standard.

1.3 Wherever a psychological service unit exists, a professional psychologist shall be responsible for planning, directing, and reviewing the provision of psychological services.

Interpretation: This psychologist shall coordinate the activities of the psychological service unit with other professional, administrative, and technical groups, both within and outside the facility. This psychologist, who may be the director, chief, or coordinator of the psychological service unit, has related responsibilities including, but not limited to, recruiting qualified staff, directing training and research activities of the service, maintaining a high level of professional and ethical practice, and assuring that staff members function only within the areas of their competency.

In order to facilitate the effectiveness of services by increasing the level of staff sensitivity and professional skills, the psychologist designated as director shall be responsible for participating in the selection of the staff and supporting personnel whose qualifications and skills (for example, language, cultural and experiential background, race, and sex) are directly relevant to the needs and characteristics of the users served.

1.4. When functioning as part of an organizational setting, professional psychologists shall bring their background and skills to bear whenever appropriate upon the goals of the organization by participating in the planning and development of overall services.[11]

Interpretation: Professional psychologists shall participate in the maintenance of high professional standards by representation on committees concerned with service delivery.

As appropriate to the setting, these activities may include active participation as voting and as officeholding members on the facility's executive, planning, and evaluation boards and committees.

1.5. Psychologists shall maintain current knowledge of scientific and professional developments that are directly related to the services they render.

Interpretation: Methods through which knowledge of scientific and professional development may be gained include, but are not limited to, continuing education, attendance at workshops, participation in staff development, and reading scientific publications.[12]

The psychologist shall have ready access to reference material related to the provision of psychological services.

Psychologists must be prepared to show evidence periodically that they are staying abreast of current knowledge and practices through continuing education.

1.6. Psychologists shall limit their practice to their demonstrated areas of professional competence.

Interpretation: Psychological services will be offered in accordance with the provider's areas of competence as defined by verifiable training and experience. When extending services beyond the range of their usual practice, psychologists shall obtain pertinent training or appropriate professional supervision.

1.7. Psychologists who wish to change their service specialty or to add an additional area of applied specialization must meet the same requirements with respect to subject matter and professional skills that apply to doctoral training in the new specialty.[13]

Interpretation: Training of doctoral-level psychologists to qualify them for change in specialty will be under the auspices of accredited university departments or professional schools that offer the doctoral degree in that specialty. Such training should be individualized, due credit being given for relevant coursework or requirements that have previously been satisfied. Merely taking an internship or acquiring experience in a practicum setting is not considered adequate preparation for becoming a clinical, counseling, industrial-organizational, or school psychologist when prior training has not been in the relevant area. Fulfillment of such an individualized training program is attested to by the award of a certificate by the supervising department or professional school indicating the successful completion of preparation in the particular specialty.

Standard 2. Programs

2.1. Composition and organization of a psychological service unit:

2.1.1. The composition and programs of a psychological service unit shall be responsive to the needs of the persons or settings served.

Interpretation: A psychological service unit shall be so structured as to facilitate effective and economical delivery of services. For example, a psychological service unit serving a predominantly low-income, ethnic, or racial minority group should have a staffing pattern and service program that is adapted to the linguistic, experiential, and attitudinal characteristics of the users.

2.1.2. A description of the organization of the psychological service unit and its lines of responsibility and accountability for the delivery of psychological services shall be available in written form to staff of the unit and to users and sanctioners on request.

Interpretation: The description should include lines of responsibility, supervisory relationships, and the level and extent of accountability for each person who provides psychological services.

2.1.3. A psychological service unit shall include sufficient numbers of professional and support personnel to achieve its goals, objectives, and purposes.

Interpretation: The work load and diversity of psychological services required and the specific goals and objectives of the setting will determine the numbers and qualifications of professional and support personnel in the psychological service unit. Where shortages in personnel exist so that psychological services cannot be rendered in a professional manner, the director of the psychological service unit shall initiate action to modify appropriately the specific goals and objectives of the service.

2.2. Policies:

2.2.1. When the psychological service unit is composed of more than one person wherein a supervisory relationship exists or is a component of a larger organization, a written statement of its objectives and scope of services shall be developed and maintained.

Interpretation: The psychological service unit shall review its objectives and scope of services annually and revise them as necessary to ensure that the psychological services offered are consistent with staff competencies and current psychological knowledge and practice. This statement should be distributed to staff and, where appropriate, to users and sanctioners on request.

2.2.2. All providers within a psychological service unit shall support the legal and civil rights of the user.[14]

Interpretation: Providers of psychological services shall safeguard the interests of the user with regard to personal, legal, and civil rights. They shall continually be sensitive to the issue of confidentiality of information, the short-term and long-term impact of their decisions and recommendations, and other matters pertaining to individual, legal, and civil rights. Concerns regarding the safeguarding of individual rights of users include, but are not limited to, problems of self-incrimination in judicial proceedings, involuntary commitment to hospitals, protection of minors or legal incompetents, discriminatory practices in employment selection procedures, recommendations for special education provisions, information relative to adverse personnel actions in the armed services, and the adjudication of domestic relations disputes in divorce and custodial proceedings. Providers of psychological services should take affirmative action by making themselves available for local committees, review boards, and similar advisory groups established to safeguard the human, civil, and legal rights of service users.

2.2.3 All providers within a psychological service unit shall be familiar with and adhere to the American Psychological Association's *Ethical Standards of Psychologists, Psychology as a Profession, Standards for Educational and Psychological Tests,* and other official policy statements relevant to standards for professional services issued by the Association.

Interpretation: Providers of psychological services, users, and sanctioners may order copies of these documents from the American Psychological Association.

2.2.4. All providers within a psychological service unit shall conform to relevant statutes established by federal, state, and local governments.

Interpretation: All providers of psychological services shall be familiar with appropriate statutes regulating the practice of psychology. They shall also be informed about agency regulations that have the force of law and that relate to the delivery of psychological services (for example, evaluation for disability retirement and special education placements). In addition, all providers shall be cognizant that federal agencies such as the Veterans Administration and the Department of Health, Education, and Welfare have policy statements regarding psychological services. Providers of psychological services shall be familiar with other statutes and regulations, including those addressed to the civil and legal rights of users (for example, those promulgated by the federal Equal Employment Opportunity Commission) that are pertinent to their scope of practice.

It shall be the responsibility of the American Psychological Association to publish periodically those federal policies, statutes, and regulations relating to this section. The state psychological associations are similarly urged to publish and distribute periodically appropriate state statutes and regulations.

> 2.2.5. All providers within a psychological service unit shall, where appropriate, inform themselves about and use the network of human services in their communities in order to link users with relevant services and resources.

Interpretation: It is incumbent on psychologists and supporting staff to be sensitive to the broader context of human needs. In recognizing the matrix of personal and societal problems, providers shall, where appropriate, make available information regarding human services such as legal aid societies, social services, employment agencies, health resources, and educational and recreational facilities. The provider of psychological services shall refer to such community resources and, when indicated, actively intervene on behalf of the user.

> 2.2.6. In the delivery of psychological services, the providers shall maintain a continuing cooperative relationship with colleagues and coworkers whenever in the best interest of the user.[15]

Interpretation: It shall be the responsibility of the psychologist to recognize the areas of special competence of other psychologists and of other professionals for either consultation or referral purposes. Providers of psychological services shall make appropriate use of other professional, technical, and administrative resources whenever these serve the best interests of the user and shall establish and maintain cooperative arrangements with such other resources as required to meet the needs of users.

2.3. Procedures:

2.3.1. Where appropriate, each psychological service unit shall be guided by a set of procedural guidelines for the delivery of psychological services. If appropriate to the setting, these guidelines shall be in written form.

Interpretation: Depending on the nature of the setting, and whenever feasible, providers should be prepared to provide a statement of procedural guidelines in either oral or written form that can be understood by users as well as sanctioners. This statement may describe the current methods, forms, procedures, and techniques being used to achieve the objectives and goals for psychological services.

This statement shall be communicated to staff and, when appropriate, to users and sanctioners. The psychological service unit shall provide for the annual review of its procedures for the delivery of psychological services.

2.3.2. Providers shall develop a plan appropriate to the provider's professional strategy of practice and to the problems presented by the user.

Interpretation: Whenever appropriate or mandated in the setting, this plan shall be in written form as a means of providing a basis for establishing accountability, obtaining informed consent, and providing a mechanism for subsequent peer review. Regardless of the type of setting or users involved, it is desirable that a plan be developed that describes the psychological services indicated and the manner in which they will be provided.[16]

A psychologist who provides services as one member of a collaborative effort shall participate in the development and implementation of the overall service plan and provide for its periodic review.

2.3.3. There shall be a mutually acceptable understanding between the provider and user or responsible agent regarding the delivery of service.

Interpretation: Varying service settings call for understandings differing in explicitness and formality. For instance, a psychologist providing services within a user organization may operate within a broad framework of understanding with this organization as a condition of employment. As another example, psychologists providing professional services to individuals in clinical, counseling, or school settings require an open-ended agreement, which specifies procedures and their known risks (if any), costs, and respective responsibilities of provider and user for achieving the agreed-on objectives.

2.3.4. Accurate, current, and pertinent documentation shall be made of essential psychological services provided.

Interpretation: Records kept of psychological services may include, but not be limited to, identifying data, dates of services, types of services, and significant actions taken. Providers of psychological services shall ensure that essential information concerning services rendered is appropriately recorded within a reasonable time of their completion.

2.3.5. Providers of psychological services shall establish a system to protect confidentiality of their records.[17]

Interpretation: Psychologists are responsible for maintaining the confidentiality of information about users of services whether obtained by themselves or by those they supervise. All persons supervised by psychologists, including nonprofessional personnel and students, who have access to records of psychological services shall be required to maintain this confidentiality as a condition of employment.

The psychologist shall not release confidential information, except with the written consent of the user directly involved or his or her legal representative. Even after the consent has been obtained for release, the psychologist should clearly identify such information as confidential to the recipient of the information.[18] If directed otherwise by statute or regulations with the force of law or by court order, the psychologist shall seek a resolution to the conflict that is both ethically and legally feasible and appropriate.

Users shall be informed in advance of any limits in the setting for maintenance of confidentiality of psychological information. For instance, psychologists in hospital settings shall inform their patients that psychological information in a patient's clinical record may be available without the patient's written consent to other members of the professional staff associated with the patient's treatment or rehabilitation. Similar limitations on confidentiality of psychological information may be present in certain school, industrial, or military settings or in instances where the user has waived confidentiality for purposes of third-party payment.

When the user intends to waive confidentiality, the psychologist should discuss the implications of releasing psychological information and assist the user in limiting disclosure only to information required by the present circumstance.

Raw psychological data (for example, test protocols, therapy or interview notes, or questionnaire returns) in which a user is identified shall be released only with the written consent of the user or legal representative and only to a person recognized by the psychologist as competent to use the data.

Any use made of psychological reports, records, or data for research or training purposes shall be consistent with this Standard. Additionally, providers of psychological services shall comply with statutory confidentiality requirements and those embodied in the American Psychological Association's *Ethical Standards of Psychologists* (American Psychological Association, 1977).

Providers of psychological services should remain sensitive to both the benefits and the possible misuse of information regarding individuals that is stored in large, computerized data banks. Providers should use their influence to ensure that such information is used in a socially responsible manner.

Standard 3. Accountability

3.1. Psychologists' professional activity shall be primarily guided by the principle of promoting human welfare.
Interpretation: Psychologists shall provide services to users in a manner that is considerate, effective, and economical.

Psychologists are responsible for making their services readily accessible to users in a manner that facilitates the user's freedom of choice.

Psychologists shall be mindful of their accountability to the sanctioners of psychological services and to the general public, provided that appropriate steps are taken to protect the confidentiality of the service relationship. In the pursuit of their professional activities, they shall aid in the conservation of human, material, and financial resources.

The psychological service unit will not withhold services to a potential client on the basis of that user's race, color, religion, sex, age, or national origin. Recognition is given, however, to the following considerations: the professional right of psychologists to limit their practice to a specific category of user (for example, children, adolescents, women); the right and responsibility of psychologists to withhold an assessment procedure when not validly applicable; the right and responsibility of psychologists to withhold evaluative, psychotherapeutic, counseling, or other services in specific instances where considerations of race, religion, color, sex, or any other difference between psychologist and client might impair the effectiveness of the relationship.[19]

Psychologists who find that psychological services are being provided in a manner that is discriminatory or exploitative to users and/or contrary to these Standards or to state or federal statutes shall take appropriate corrective action, which may include the refusal to provide services. When conflicts of interest arise, the psychologist shall be guided in the resolution of differences by the principles set forth in the *Ethical Standards of Psychologists* of the American Psychological Association and by the "Guidelines for Conditions of Employment of Psychologists" (1972).[20]

3.2. Psychologists shall pursue their activities as members of an independent, autonomous profession.[21]

Interpretation: Psychologists shall be aware of the implications of their activities for the profession as a whole. They shall seek to eliminate discriminatory practices instituted for self-serving purposes that are not in the interest of the user (for example, arbitrary requirements for referral and supervision by another profession). They shall be cognizant of their responsibilities for the development of the profession, participate where possible in the training and career development of students and other providers, participate as appropriate in the training of paraprofessionals, and integrate and supervise their contributions within the structure established for delivering psychological services. Where appropriate, they shall facilitate the development of, and participate in, professional standards review mechanisms.[22]

Psychologists shall seek to work with other professionals in a cooperative manner for the good of the user and the benefit of the general public. Psychologists associated with multidisciplinary settings shall support the principle that members of each participating profession shall have equal rights and opportunities to share all privileges and responsibilities of full membership in the human service facility and to administer service programs in their respective areas of competence.

3.3 There shall be periodic, systematic, and effective evaluations of psychological services.[23]

Interpretation: When the psychological service unit is a component of a larger organization, regular assessment of progress in achieving goals shall be provided in the service delivery plan, including consideration of the effectiveness of psychological services relative to costs in terms of time, money, and the availability of professional and support personnel.

Evaluation of the efficiency and effectiveness of the psychological service delivery system should be conducted internally and, when possible, under independent auspices.

It is highly desirable that there be a periodic reexamination of review mechanisms to ensure that these attempts at public safeguards are effective and cost efficient and do not place unnecessary encumbrances on the provider or unnecessary additional expense to users or sanctioners for services rendered.

3.4. Psychologists are accountable for all aspects of the services they provide and shall be responsive to those concerned with these services.[24]

Interpretation: In recognizing their responsibilities to users, sanctioners, third-party purchasers, and other providers, wherever appropriate and consistent with the user's legal rights and privileged communications, psychologists shall make available information about, and opportunity to participate in, decisions concerning such issues, as initiation, termination, continuation, modification, and evaluation of psychological services. Additional copies of these *Standards for Providers of Psychological Services* can be ordered from the American Psychological Association.

Depending on the settings, accurate and full information shall be made available to prospective individual or organization users regarding the qualifications of providers, the nature and extent of services offered, and, where appropriate, financial and social costs.

Where appropriate, psychologists shall inform users of their payment policies and their willingness to assist in obtaining reimbursement. Those who accept reimbursement from a third party should be acquainted with the appropriate statutes and regulations and should instruct their users on proper procedures for submitting claims and limits on confidentiality of claims information, in accordance with pertinent statutes.

Standard 4. Environment

4.1. Providers of psychological services shall promote the development in the service setting of a physical, organizational, and social environment that facilitates optimal human functioning.
Interpretation: Federal, state, and local requirements for safety, health, and sanitation must be observed. Attention shall be given to the comfort and, where relevant, to the privacy of providers and users.

As providers of services, psychologists have the responsibility to be concerned with the environment of their service unit, especially as it affects the quality of service, but also as it impinges on human functioning in the larger unit or organization when the service unit is included in such a larger context. Physical arrangements and organizational policies and procedures should be conducive to the human dignity, self-respect, and optimal functioning of users and to the effective delivery of service. The atmosphere in which psychological services are rendered should be appropriate to the service and to the users, whether in office, clinic, school, or industrial organization.

Notes

1. Members of the Task Force on Standards for Service Facilities that submitted the original Standards in September 1974 were Milton L. Blum, Jacqueline C. Bouhoutsos, Jerry H. Clark, Harold A. Edgerton, Marian D. Hall, Durand F. Jacobs (chair, 1972–1974), Floyd H. Martinez, John E. Muthard, Asher R. Pacht, William D. Pierce, Sue A. Warren, and Alfred M. Wellner (chair, 1970–1971). Staff liaisons from the APA Office of Professional Affairs were John J. McMillan (1970–1971), Gottlieb C. Simon (1971–1973), and Arthur Centor (1973–1974). Reprinted from the *American Psychologist,* 1977, *32,* 495–505.

2. The footnotes appended to these Standards represent an attempt to provide a coherent context of other policy statements of the Association regarding professional practice. The Standards extend these previous policy statements where necessary to reflect current concerns of the public and the profession.

3. NIMH Grant MH 21696.

4. For the purpose of transition, persons who met the following criteria on or before the date of adoption of the original Standards on September 4, 1974, shall also be considered professional psychologists: (1) a master's degree from a program primarily psychological in content from a regionally accredited university or professional school; (2) appropriate education, training, and experience in the area of service offered; (3) a license or certificate in the state in which they practice, conferred by a state board of psychological examiners, or the endorsement of the state psychological association through voluntary certification, or, for practice in primary and secondary schools, a state department of education certificate as a school psychologist provided that the certificate required at least two graduate years.

5. Minutes of the Board of Professional Affairs meeting, Washington, D.C., March 8–9, 1974.

6. This definition is less restrictive than Recommendation 4 of the APA (1967) policy statement setting forth model state legislation affecting the practice of psychology (hereinafter referred to as State Guidelines), proposing one level for state license or certificate and "requiring the doctoral degree from an accredited university or college in a program that is primarily psychological, and no less than two years of supervised experience, one of which is subsequent to the granting of the doctoral degree. This level should be designated by the title of 'psychologist'" (p. 1099).

The 1972 APA "Guidelines for Conditions of Employment of Psychologists" (hereinafter referred to as CEP Guidelines) introduces slightly different shadings of meaning in its section on "Standards for Entry into the Profession" as follows:

> Persons are properly identified as psychologists when they have completed the training and experience recognized as necessary to perform functions consistent with one of the several levels in a career in psychology. This training includes possession of a degree earned in a program primarily psychological in content. In the case of psychological practice, it involves services for a fee, appropriate registration, certification, or licensing as provided by laws of the state in which the practices will apply [American Psychological Association, 1972, p. 331].

In some situations, specialty designations and standards may be relevant. The National Register of Health Service Providers in Psychology, which based its criteria on this standard, identifies qualified psychologists in the health services field.

7. As noted in the opening section of these Standards, functions and activities of psychologists relating to the teaching of psychology, the writing or editing of scholarly or scientific manuscripts, and the conduct of scientific research do not fall within the purview of these Standards.

8. These definitions should be compared to the State Guidelines, which include definitions of *psychologist* and the *practice of psychology* as follows:

> Persons represent themselves to be psychologists when they hold themselves out to the public by any title or description of services incorporating the words *psychology, psychological, psychologist,* and/or offer to render or render services as defined below to individuals, groups, organizations, or the public for a fee, monetary or otherwise.
>
> The practice of psychology within the meaning of this act is defined as rendering to individuals, groups or organizations, or the public any psychological service involving the application of principles, methods, and procedures of understanding, predicting, and influencing behavior, such as the principles pertaining to learning, perception, motivation, thinking, emotions, and interpersonal relationships; the methods and procedures of interviewing, counseling, and psychotherapy; of constructing, administering, and interpreting tests of mental abilities, aptitudes, interests, attitudes, personality characteristics, emotions, and motivation; and of assessing public opinion.
>
> The application of said principles and methods includes but is not restricted to diagnosis, prevention, and amelioration of adjustment problems and emotional and mental disorders of individuals and groups; hypnosis; educational and vocational counseling; personnel selection and management; the evaluation and planning for effective work and learning situations; advertising and market research; and the resolution of interpersonal and social conflicts.
>
> The word *psychotherapy* within the meaning of this act means the use of learning, conditioning methods, and emotional reactions, in a professional relationship, to assist a person or persons to modify feelings, atti-

> tudes, and behavior that are intellectually, socially, or emotionally maladjustive or ineffectual.
>
> The practice of psychology shall be as defined above, any existing statute in the state of —— to the contrary notwithstanding [American Psychological Association, 1967, pp. 1098–1099].

9. The relation of a psychological service unit to a larger facility or institution is also addressed indirectly in the CEP Guidelines, which emphasize the roles, responsibilities, and prerogatives of the psychologist when he or she is employed by or provides services for another agency, institution, or business.

10. This Standard replaces earlier recommendations in the 1967 State Guidelines concerning exemption of psychologists from licensure. Recommendations 8 and 9 of those Guidelines read as follows:

> 8. Persons employed as psychologists by accredited academic institutions, governmental agencies, research laboratories, and business corporations should be exempted, provided such employees are performing those duties for which they are employed by such organizations, and within the confines of such organizations.
> 9. Persons employed as psychologists by accredited academic institutions, governmental agencies, research laboratories, and business corporations consulting or offering their research findings or providing scientific information to like organizations for a fee should be exempted [American Psychological Association, 1967, p. 1100].

On the other hand, the 1967 State Guidelines specifically denied exemptions under certain conditions, as noted in Recommendations 10 and 11:

> 10. Persons employed as psychologists who offer or provide psychological services to the public for a fee,

over and above the salary that they receive for the performance of their regular duties, should not be exempted.

11. Persons employed as psychologists by organizations that sell psychological services to the public should not be exempted [American Psychological Association, 1967, pp. 1100–1101].

The present APA policy, as reflected in this Standard, establishes a single code of practice for psychologists, providing covered services to users in any setting. The present minimum requirement is that a psychologist providing any covered service must meet local statutory requirements for licensure or certification. See the section "Principles and Implications of the Standards" for an elaboration of this position.

11. A closely related principle is found in the APA (1972) CEP Guidelines:

> It is the policy of APA that psychology as an independent profession is entitled to parity with other health and human service professions in institutional practices and before the law. Psychologists in interdisciplinary settings such as colleges and universities, medical schools, clinics, private practice groups, and other agencies expect parity with other professions in such matters as academic rank, board status, salaries, fringe benefits, fees, participation in administrative decisions, and all other conditions of employment, private contractual arrangements, and status before the law and legal institutions [American Psychological Association, 1972, p. 333].

12. See CEP Guidelines (section entitled "Career Development") for a closely related statement:

> Psychologists are expected to encourage institutions and agencies that employ them to sponsor or con-

> duct career development programs. The purpose of these programs would be to enable psychologists to engage in study for professional advancement and to keep abreast of developments in their field [American Psychological Association, 1972, p. 332].

13. This Standard follows closely the statement regarding "Policy on Training for Psychologists Wishing to Change Their Specialty" adopted by the APA Council of Representatives in January 1976. Included therein was the implementing provision that "this policy statement shall be incorporated in the guidelines of the Committee on Accreditation so that appropriate sanctions can be brought to bear on university and internship training programs that violate [it]."

14. See also APA's (1977) *Ethical Standards of Psychologists,* especially Principles 5 (confidentiality), 6 (welfare of the consumer), and 9 (pursuit of research activities); and see *Ethical Principles in the Conduct of Research with Human Participants* [American Psychological Association, 1973a].

15. Support for this position is found in the section in *Psychology as a Profession* on relations with other professions:

> Professional persons have an obligation to know and take into account the traditions and practices of other professional groups with whom they work and to cooperate fully with members of such groups with whom research, service, and other functions are shared [American Psychological Association, 1968, p. 5].

16. One example of a specific application of this principle is found in Guideline 2 in APA's (1973b, p. 933) "Guidelines for Psychologists Conducting Growth Groups":

> The following information should be made available in *writing* [italics added] to all prospective participants:
>
> 1. An explicit statement of the purpose of the group.
> 2. Types of techniques that may be employed.

3. The education, training and experience of the leader or leaders.
4. The fee and any additional expense that may be incurred.
5. A statement as to whether or not a follow-up service is included in the fee.
6. Goals of the group experience and techniques to be used.
7. Amounts and kinds of responsibility to be assumed by the leader and by the participants. For example, (a) the degree to which a participant is free not to follow suggestions and prescriptions of the group leader and other group members; (b) any restrictions on a participant's freedom to leave the group at any time.
8. Issues of confidentiality.

17. See again Principle 5 (confidentiality) in *Ethical Standards of Psychologists* [American Psychological Association, 1977].

18. Support for the principle of privileged communication is found in at least two policy statements of the Association:

> In the interest of both the public and the client and in accordance with the requirements of good professional practice, the profession of psychology seeks recognition of the privileged nature of confidential communications with clients, preferably through statutory enactment or by administrative policy where more appropriate [American Psychological Association, 1968, p. 8].

25. Wherever possible, a clause protecting the privileged nature of the psychologist-client relationship be included.
26. When appropriate, psychologists assist in obtaining general "across the board" legislation for such privileged communications [American Psychological Association, 1967, p. 1103].

19. This paragraph is drawn directly from the CEP Guidelines [American Psychological Association, 1972, p. 333].

20. "It is recognized that under certain circumstances the interests and goals of a particular community or segment of interest in the population may be in conflict with the general welfare. Under such circumstances, the psychologist's professional activity must be primarily guided by the principle of promoting human welfare" [American Psychological Association, 1972, p. 334].

21. Support for the principle of the independence of psychology as a profession is found in the following:

> As members of an autonomous profession, psychologists reject limitations on their freedom of thought and action other than those imposed by their moral, legal, and social responsibilities. The Association is always prepared to provide appropriate assistance to any responsible members who become subjected to unreasonable limitations on their opportunity to function as practitioners, teachers, researchers, administrators, or consultants. The Association is always prepared to cooperate with any responsible professional organization in opposing any unreasonable limitations on the professional functions of the members of that organization.
>
> This insistence on professional autonomy has been upheld over the years by the affirmative actions of the courts and other public and private bodies in support of the right of psychologists—and other professionals—to pursue those functions for which they are trained and qualified to perform [American Psychological Association, 1968, p. 9].
>
> Organized psychology has the responsibility to define and develop its own profession, consistent with the general canons of science and with the public welfare.
>
> Psychologists recognize that other professions and other groups will, from time to time, seek to define the roles and responsibilities of psychologists. The APA

> opposes such developments on the same principles that it is opposed to the psychological profession taking positions which would define the work and scope of responsibility of other duly recognized professions [American Psychological Association, 1972, p. 333].

22. APA support for peer review is detailed in the following excerpt from the APA (1971) statement entitled "Psychology and National Health Care":

> All professions participating in a national health plan should be directed to establish review mechanisms (or performance evaluations) that include not only peer review but active participation by persons representing the consumer. In situations where there are fiscal agents, they should also have representation when appropriate [p. 1026].

23. This standard on program evaluation is based directly on the following excerpts of two APA position papers:

> The quality and availability of health services should be evaluated continuously by both consumers and health professionals. Research into the efficiency and effectiveness of the system should be conducted both internally and under independent auspices [American Psychological Association, 1971, p. 1025].
>
> The comprehensive community mental health center should devote an explicit portion of its budget to program evaluation. All centers should inculcate in their staff attention to and respect for research findings; the larger centers have an obligation to set a high priority on basic research and to give formal recognition to research as a legitimate part of the duties of staff members.
>
> Only by explicit appraisal of program effects can worthy approaches be retained and refined, ineffective ones dropped. Evaluative monitoring of program

> achievements may vary, of course, from the relatively informal to the systematic and quantitative, depending on the importance of the issue, the availability of resources, and the willingness of those responsible to take the risks of substituting informed judgment for evidence [Smith and Hobbs, 1966, pp. 21–22].

24. See also the CEP Guidelines for the following statement: "Psychologists recognize that . . . they alone are accountable for the consequences and effects of their services, whether as teachers, researchers, or practitioners. This responsibility cannot be shared, delegated, or reduced" [American Psychological Association, 1972, p. 334].

References

Accreditation Council for Facilities for the Mentally Retarded. *Standards for Residential Facilities for the Mentally Retarded,* Chicago, Ill.: Joint Commission on Accreditation of Hospitals, 1971.

American Psychological Association, Committee on Legislation. "A Model for State Legislation Affecting the Practice of Psychology 1967." *American Psychologist,* 1967, *22,* 1095–1103.

American Psychological Association. *Psychology as a Profession.* Washington, D.C.: American Psychological Association, 1968.

American Psychological Association. "Psychology and National Health Care." *American Psychologist,* 1971, *26,* 1025–1026.

American Psychological Association. "Guidelines for Conditions of Employment of Psychologists." *American Psychologist,* 1972, *27,* 331–334.

American Psychological Association. *Ethical Principles in the Conduct of Research with Human Participants.* Washington, D.C.: American Psychological Association, 1973a.

American Psychological Association. "Guidelines for Psychologists Conducting Growth Groups." *American Psychologist,* 1973b, *28,* 933.

American Psychological Association. *Standards for Educational and*

Psychological Tests. Washington, D.C.: American Psychological Association, 1974.

American Psychological Association. *Ethical Standards of Psychologists: 1977 Revision*. Washington, D.C.: American Psychological Association, 1977.

Joint Commission on Accreditation of Hospitals. *Accreditation Manual for Psychiatric Facilities 1972*. Chicago, Ill.: Joint Commission on Accreditation of Hospitals, 1972.

SMITH, M. B., and HOBBS, N. *The Community and the Community Mental Health Center*. Washington, D.C.: American Psychological Association, 1966.

Ethical and Legal Issues Related to Psychological Interventions: A Selected Annotated Bibliography

Stephanie B. Stolz

Ethics of Behavior Modification

BANDURA, A. "The Ethics and Social Purposes of Behavior Modification." In C. M. Franks and G. T. Wilson (Eds.), *Annual Review of Behavior Therapy Theory and Practice: 1975.* Vol. 3. New York: Brunner/Mazel, 1975.

This thoughtful and thought-provoking article discusses behavior modification-related ethical issues in their social context.

The author notes that all psychotherapies, including behavior modification, tend to be used to foster what is culturally valued. Practitioners of all persuasions are reinforced more powerfully for using their knowledge and skills in the service of existing systems than for changing them, so that idealistic and socially oriented efforts are difficult to sustain. The author says that if psychologists are to have a significant impact on life's common problems they must apply their technology to detrimental social practices, rather than limiting themselves to treating the casualties of those social practices.

BROWN, B. S., WIENCKOWSKI, L. A., and STOLZ, S. B. *Behavior Modification: Perspective on a Current Issue.* DHEW Publication No. (ADM)75–202. Washington, D.C.: U.S. Government Printing Office, 1975.

This report enunciates the policy of the National Institute of Mental Health with respect to behavior modification. The pamphlet also describes briefly the major behavior modification methods, reviews some of the evidence for the efficacy of the techniques, and deals with the major ethical issues, with sections devoted to the use of behavior modification in prisons and to the implications for behavior modification of recent litigation. The authors call for continued monitoring of behavior modification by the public and for further research on behavioral technology.

BRUCH, H. "Perils of Behavior Modification in Treatment of Anorexia Nervosa." *Journal of the American Medical Association,* 1974, *230,* 1419–1422.

The author, a distinguished psychotherapist with extensive experience in treating anorexia nervosa, criticizes the use of behavior modification treatment for that problem because, in her opinion, it prevents patients from developing a sense of inner psychic control, competence, and self-directed identity and from developing a sense of initiative, self-esteem, autonomy, or self-determination. She supports this critique with three case histories. The author's conclusion is that recognizable personality difficulties represent a definite contraindication for the use of behavior modification in the treatment of anorexia nervosa.

CARRERA, F., III, and ADAMS, P. L. "An Ethical Perspective on Operant Conditioning." *Journal of the American Academy of Child Psychiatry,* 1970, *9,* 607–623.

Written from the point of view of child psychiatry and psychodynamic psychotherapy, this article is sharply critical of behavior modification, which it characterizes as limited, impersonal, paternalistic, and mechanistic, as well as often in conflict with the child's best interests. The authors praise child psychotherapy as being nondoctrinaire, flexible, and sensitive, and serving the entire range of the child's interests. Behavior modification techniques can be used by child psychotherapists, however, in combination with other techniques; an example of such a case is described.

ERICKSON, R. C. "Walden III: Toward an Ethics of Changing Behavior." *Journal of Religion and Health,* 1977, *16,* 7–14.

People are continually involved in a process of reciprocal influence and hence are responsible for the effect of their actions on others, regardless of the unplanned or unintentional nature of that effect. In this context, behavior modification and other psychological therapies are viewed as therapists' managing their own behavior in such a way as to enable clients to change theirs. The author contends it is an error to place either the individual or the community at the center of ethical decisions; rather, responsible ethical decisions in the author's model involve both the individual and the community; individuals choose for themselves and for the group they are a part of, and the community decides what is good for it and the individuals who are involved. In this model, neither the individual nor the community can impose their will on the other, because both must agree. Behavior modification requires new ethical decisions; the author contends that an ethical policy based on individualism or conformity is doomed to inevitable failure. Using behavior modification so that both individuals and the community are enhanced can lead to growth and development.

HALLECK, S. L. "Legal and Ethical Aspects of Behavior Control." *American Journal of Psychiatry,* 1974, *131,* 381–385.

Noting that the increasing effectiveness of psychiatric treatment, especially behavior therapy, has led to a new climate of concern over behavior control, the author urges psychiatrists to develop a system of internal control and monitoring of psychiatric practice to protect the rights of patients while enabling treatment of those who will benefit from it. The discussion is focused on the need for truly informed consent and safeguards such as the use of a professional review board or monitoring agency in those instances where the patients do not consent to the treatment and yet are judged dangerous to themselves or others and incompetent to evaluate the necessity for treatment and where the professionals believe the treatment is likely to benefit the patients and those around them. Other problem situations are discussed, including issues that arise when consent is obtained under duress and subtle political issues relating to voluntary patients.

HOLLAND, J. G. "Behavior Modification for Prisoners, Patients, and Other People as a Prescription for the Planned Society." *Mexican Journal of the Analysis of Behavior,* 1975, *1,* 81–95.

Several behavioral programs, such as Special Treatment and Rehabilitative Training project (START), Contingencies Applicable to Special Education (CASE), and Emery Air Freight, are criticized because, in the author's view, minor or modest reinforcers were used in the programs to control the behavior of the participants, with sizable gains for the institution doing the controlling. Behavior control contains the potential for invading privacy and violating other basic human rights when the professional is responsible to some third person or an organization, rather than to the client. The author contends that manipulation is not a necessary consequence of applications of behavioral technology but notes that professionals find it difficult to work for objectives different from or contrary to those of the persons or institutions who hire them. Suggestions are offered as to the sort of technology that a socially concerned behavioral professional might develop, such as systems to reinforce prison staff for prisoners' low recidivism rates. However, the author says we must ultimately find some third type of technique that does not manipulate anyone toward others' goals but rather is controlled by those who are undergoing behavior change. The author's ideal is an egalitarian, nonexploitative, cooperative society, a model for which is Fairweather's lodge system for released chronic mental patients.

LONDON, P. *Behavior Control.* New York: Harper & Row, 1969. (Revised second edition, Meridian Books, 1977.)

In a brief, elegantly written book, the author examines the major technologies for behavior control and assesses their effectiveness and potential for future development. The book includes an extended discussion of practical and ethical considerations related to behavioral technology. This book is a pioneer effort in the area of discussions of ethics and behavior modification; the rest of us are only now coming to the ideas presented so vividly by London in 1969.

O'LEARY, S. G., and O'LEARY, K. D. "Ethical Issues of Behavior Modification Research in Schools." *Psychology in the Schools,* 1977, *14,* 299–307.

Focusing on research using behavior modification techniques and conducted in public schools, this article discusses issues of informed consent, determination of classroom goals, legitimacy of rewards and aversive controls in the classroom, conceptions of behavior modification as manipulative and mechanistic, who can implement the procedures, research design, and accountability. The authors conclude that issues regarding the protection of human subjects in behavior modification research are no different from those in other treatment-oriented research with children; parents and teachers share the responsibility of preventing misuse of behavior modification procedures. The authors present some suggested guidelines and principles for the conduct of research in the classroom. The article is based on testimony to the National Commission for the Protection of Human Subjects of Biomedical and Behavioral Research.

PAGE, S., CARON, P., and YATES, E. "Behavior Modification Methods and Institutional Psychology." *Professional Psychology,* 1975, *6,* 175–181.

The authors speculate that in order to get behavioral procedures adopted by the staff of mental hospitals, psychologists permitted them to be used to reinforce patients for such uninspiring achievements as brushing their teeth and to penalize patients for minor rule transgressions. One result, in the authors' view, is that insufficient attention has been given to the choice of the goals of behavioral programs, and, more broadly, to the selection of the goals for the entire mental health system. Behavior modification is potentially the most creative therapeutic modality, the authors say, and ideally enables clinicians to permit the patient to choose the behavior to be changed and the goal of therapy.

ROOS, P. "Human Rights and Behavior Modification." *Mental Retardation,* 1974, *12* (3), 3–6.

Behavior modification and other therapeutic and educational approaches raise common ethical issues relating to the use of aversive conditioning, control of behavior, and selection of goals. The author contends, however, that behavior modification is more vulnerable than other change strategies, and he suggests some principles and guidelines whose adoption might minimize criticism and harmonize behavioral practice with prevailing cultural values.

STOLZ, S. B. "Ethics of Social and Educational Interventions: Historical Context and a Behavioral Analysis." In T. A. Brigham and A. C. Catania (Eds.), *Handbook of Applied Behavior Research: Social and Instructional Processes.* New York: Irvington-Neiburg/Wiley, in press.

The first part of this chapter presents an extended historical background for the concern about ethics in behavior modification, beginning with the post-World War II period. The second portion of the chapter analyzes ethical concepts in behavioral terms and reviews in detail the process of decision making prior to the initiation of an intervention, spelling out the classes of behavior involved and potential individual and societal reinforcers for those classes of behavior. The concept of countercontrol plays an important part in this analysis. The author's goal is to develop principles of ethics that are consistent with the approach of applied behavior analysis.

ULRICH, R. "Behavior Control and Public Concern." *Psychological Record,* 1967, *17,* 229–234.

Justified and unjustified causes for alarm over behavior control are discussed. The author concludes that, since behavior control is a fact, the best course of action is to educate people so that they understand how their behavior is controlled and can exercise self-control.

U.S. Congress, Senate, Committee on the Judiciary, Subcommittee on Constitutional Rights. *Individual Rights and the Federal Role in Behavior Modification.* 93rd Cong., 2d sess., November 1974. Washington, D.C.: U.S. Government Printing Office, 1974.

This 651-page compendium includes a statement by Senator Sam J. Ervin, Jr. on the dangers of behavior modification, an overview of the extent of federal involvement, detailed descriptions of every behavior modification program supported at the time by the federal government, and some denials from administrators like the director of the National Science Foundation that their agencies are supporting projects in which behavior is being modified. The report also includes materials ordinarily difficult to obtain, for example, court decisions in major cases like *Wyatt, Knecht, Kaimowitz,* and *Clonce* v. *Richardson* (the START case), Wexler's (1973) "Token and Taboo" article, and the Nuremberg Code.

Litigation Related to Behavior Modification

BUDD, K. S., and BAER, D. M. "Behavior Modification and the Law: Implications of Recent Judicial Decisions." *Journal of Psychiatry & Law,* 1976, *4,* 171–244.

The courts have displayed an unprecedented interest in

articulating the rights of institutionalized residents and establishing specific standards to ensure that these rights are protected. This article examines the intersection of behavior modification and this recent litigation, especially that dealing with prisoners and mentally handicapped persons. The authors contend that some of the emerging standards might limit the use of certain behavior modification techniques, even to the extent that necessary therapeutic interventions could be delayed or prohibited. The article presents a comprehensive review of the court decisions relating to behavior modification procedures, outlines some of the complex and largely unresolved issues raised by the decisions, and suggests some solutions to these problems from the viewpoint of behavioral psychologists.

FRIEDMAN, P. R. "Legal Regulation of Applied Behavior Analysis in Mental Institutions and Prisons." *Arizona Law Review,* 1975, *17,* 39–104.

This article analyzes the legal limitations on behavior modification, focusing especially on the client's right to refuse treatment. Although the author says he is using behavior modification as an example and that the conclusions apply equally to other interventions, the implication throughout is that behavior modification poses special problems not raised by other therapies. On the basis of a detailed discussion of relevant statutory law, common law, and constitutional principles, the author draws specific implications for the conduct of token economy programs and deals with issues such as the determination of competency and of the voluntariness of consent. The appendices include proposed standards and procedures to govern applied behavior analysis in mental institutions and an example of the application of those standards to a hypothetical case.

GOLDIAMOND, I. "Singling Out Behavior Modification for Legal Regulation: Some Effects on Patient Care, Psychotherapy, and Research in General." *Arizona Law Review,* 1975, *17,* 105–126.

In a critique of Friedman (1975), the author contends that if behavior modification were singled out for regulation the quality of treatment available for patients may be detrimentally affected because of the many bureaucratic barriers that would be posed solely for behavior modification practice. Further, he contends that the standards and procedures proposed by Friedman would adversely affect scientific research because novel procedures would presumably not be approved for trial in the absence of evidence for their effectiveness.

HELDMAN, A. W. "Social Psychology Versus the First Amendment Freedoms, Due-Process Liberty, and Limited Government." *Cumberland-Samford Law Review,* 1973, *4,* 1–40.

Essentially an extended book review of Skinner's (1971) *Beyond Freedom and Dignity,* the article also touches on and severely criticizes the behavior modification practices of the Huntsville-Madison County Mental Health Center. The author, a lawyer, criticizes behavior modification for its intrusion on freedom, Skinner for his behavioral analysis of freedom and dignity, and the Mental Health Center for imposing community norms on the clients' behavior. The critique is based on the freedoms stated in the First and Ninth Amendments to the Constitution.

KASSIRER, L. B. "Behavior Modification for Patients and Prisoners: Constitutional Ramifications of Enforced Therapy." *Journal of Psychiatry & Law,* 1974, *2,* 245–302.

KASSIRER, L. B. "The Right to Treatment and the Right to Refuse Treatment—Recent Case Law." *Journal of Psychiatry & Law,* 1974, *2,* 455–470.

The author of these two articles begins by noting the encouraging results reported in outcome studies of behavior modification and says that behavior modification appears to entail no dangers beyond those inherent in any institutional treatment method. The papers then concentrate on the relation of behavior therapy practice in hospitals and prisons and relevant current litigation, particularly *Donaldson* v. *O'Connor,* a case dealing with the right to treatment, and *Clonce* v. *Richardson,* the START case relating to the right to refuse treatment. A wide range of legal issues applicable to behavior modification is covered in some depth.

MARTIN, R. *Legal Challenges to Behavior Modification.* Champaign, Ill.: Research Press, 1975.

Court decisions in the last few years have been increasingly concerned with mental health interventions. The developing mental health case law reflects societal concern about civil liberties, accountability, and the rights of disadvantaged groups, including mental patients, the mentally retarded, and prisoners. This book reviews the implications of these cases for mental health intervention programs in public institutions. The author describes the circumstances under which such programs could be challenged legally and suggests how professionals could design programs that would not interfere with clients' rights and how clients could obtain the best possible treatment. The legal issues discussed are relevant to all mental health interventions, not only to behavior modification. The lengthy checklist of questions provided can be used to evaluate any mental health program in a public institution to ensure that clients' rights are not being interfered with.

SPECE, R. G., JR. "Conditioning and Other Technologies Used to 'Treat?' 'Rehabilitate?' 'Demolish?' Prisoners and Mental Patients." *Southern California Law Review,* 1972, *45,* 616–684.

Several types of interventions are described briefly, including psychosocial interventions, chemotherapy, and psychosurgery; the use of Anectine in several California institutions is described in detail. The article also summarizes the legal basis, for prisoners and mental patients, of a right to treatment and a right to refuse treatment. The author proposes some guidelines for deciding which treatments should be included in a right to refuse treatment. Problems in obtaining truly informed consent and legal remedies if rights are violated are also discussed.

TRYON, W. W. "Behavior Modification Therapy and the Law." *Professional Psychology,* 1976, *7,* 468–474.

According to this article, behavioral professionals are more likely to be sued for malpractice because, among other reasons, of the specificity of behavior modification therapies and the fact that we live in an increasingly litigious society. To warn behavioral practitioners, the author presents a discussion of key issues related to informed consent, accountability, and due process as they affect the practice of behavior modification.

WEXLER, D. B. "Token and Taboo: Behavior Modification, Token Economies, and the Law." *California Law Review,* 1973, *61,* 81–109.

A classic article in which the author draws out the possible implications of the *Wyatt* v. *Stickney* decision for the practice of behavior modification, specifically token economies in mental institutions. The *Wyatt* ruling did not specifically mention behavior modification, and the author's application of that ruling to token economies has had major impact on the conduct of token programs.

WEXLER, D. B. "Behavior Modification and Legal Developments." *American Behavioral Scientist,* 1975, *18,* 679–684.

This article presents a brief overview of the major cases related to some form of behavior modification, especially the use of aversive techniques. The author raises a number of searching and as yet unresolved questions on basic concerns relating to informed consent, the use of deprivation, and the selection of target behavior.

Behavior Modification in Prisons

Comptroller General of the United States. *Behavior Modification Programs: The Bureau of Prisons' Alternative to Long Term Segregation.* Report No. GGD-75-73. August 5, 1975.

The Bureau of Prisons attempted to avoid long-term segregation of problem prisoners by instituting behavior modification programs aimed at making prisoners more amenable to institutional discipline and more receptive to rehabilitation activities. After a review of several such programs, this General Accounting Office report concludes that the Bureau of Prisons did not manage its behavioral programs well: It assessed neither the need for the special programs nor their overall operations or results. Several recommendations are made for future improvements in program management and monitoring.

GOLDBERGER, D. "Court Challenges to Prison Behavior Modification Programs: A Case Study." *American Criminal Law Review,* 1975, *13,* 37–68.

This article analyzes the conduct of a case, *Armstrong* v. *Bensinger,* challenging the constitutionality of an inmate "behavior modification program" in Illinois. The Special Program Unit, whose practices were the origin of the complaint, used, as did the Patuxent Institution, "behavior modification" in only a loose sense. Specific responses were not reinforced; rather, after an initial harsh deprivation, privileges were expanded if an inmate's conduct remained "satisfactory" for thirty consecutive days; further thirty-day periods of acceptable behavior resulted in additional increases in privileges and finally in being returned to the general prison population. Although psychiatric testimony during the trial emphasized that the program did not approximate known models of behavior modification, the case is still considered by the author of the article to exemplify litigation on prison behavior modification programs.

HOBBS, T. R., and HOLT, M. M. "The Effects of Token Reinforcement on the Behavior of Delinquents in Cottage Settings." *Journal of Applied Behavior Analysis,* 1976, *9,* 189–198.

MILAN, M. A., and MCKEE, J. M. "The Cellblock Token Economy: Token Reinforcement Procedures in a Maximum Security Correctional Institution for Adult Male Felons." *Journal of Applied Behavior Analysis.* 1976, *9,* 253–275.

These two reports of experimental behavioral modification programs share a common comment on ethics: In both programs, the administration of the institution wanted the researchers to begin by choosing targets that would be convenient for the staff and would meet the requirements of institutional management; preparation for community living came later in the administration's hierarchy of program outcomes. Both groups of researchers note that they could have refused to use the program to adjust the inmates to the prison setting and that the cost of so refusing would be loss of permission to intervene at all.

KENNEDY, R. E. "Behavior Modification in Prisons." In W. E. Craighead, A. E. Kazdin, and M. J. Mahoney (Eds.), *Behavior Modification: Principles, Issues, and Applications.* Boston: Houghton Mifflin, 1976.

This chapter describes the procedures and reported results of the major behavior modification programs in prisons, including START, the Patuxent Institution, and the program at Draper Correctional Center in Alabama, and evaluates each program in the context of the data, legal decisions, and expert testimony from behavioral professionals. The ethical issues relevant to the use of behavior modification in prison are discussed. The author notes that the powerful use their access to reinforcers to direct intervention programs to support the status quo and that resources are lacking to support the dissemination of behavioral technology to the powerless in an attempt to improve their material and political lot.

MILAN, M. A., and MCKEE, J. M. "Behavior Modification: Principles and Applications in Corrections." In D. Glaser (Ed.), *Handbook of Criminology.* Chicago: Rand McNally, 1974.

The authors directed the development of a programmed instructional system for use in prisons' academic and vocational programs. The program was implemented at Draper Correctional Center in Alabama. This chapter gives basic definitions of operant conditioning terminology and describes some behavior modification techniques. Several programs, including the authors' own program, are described and evaluated in terms of outcome data. They conclude that the beneficial effects of token programs within prisons will be short-lived unless transitional and community-based programs follow up on the results.

OPTON, E. M., JR. "Psychiatric Violence Against Prisoners: When Therapy Is Punishment." *Mississippi Law Journal,* 1974, *45,* 605–644.

A distinction is commonly made between treatment and punishment. The author contends that maintaining this distinction when describing interventions in prisons permits mental health personnel to become involved in "violence" against prisoners under the guise of treatment. His argument rests on his definition of *treatment* as something done at the request of a patient and *punishment* as something done against a person's will. If one assumes, in addition, that voluntary consent is not possible for an institutionalized person, it follows that any intervention in a prison is *punishment,* by the author's definition. Examples of specific programs in prisons are given, including START.

U.S. Congress, House, Committee on the Judiciary, Subcommittee on Courts, Civil Liberties, and the Administration of Justice. *Oversight Hearing: Behavior Modification Programs in the Federal Bureau of Prisons.* 93rd Cong., 2d sess., 27 February 1974 (Serial No. 26). Washington, D.C.: U.S. Government Printing Office, 1974.

The hearing reported in this pamphlet was called because of the concerns expressed about the START program. Several federal officials' testimony is included, including that of the director of the Federal Bureau of Prisons, who notes the difficulty of defining behavior modification and hence of identifying which programs are and are not "behavior modification programs." Asked how he would prevent some of the problems of START from affecting future Bureau of Prisons programs, the director responded that he would not use the term *behavioral modification,* but would emphasize the everyday use of positive rewards and motivation. The report includes a detailed description of the START program and a proposal for the Morgantown program, which was later implemented, as well as for the Butner program, which was not.

General Ethical Issues

ARGYRIS, C. "Dangers in Applying Results from Experimental Social Psychology." *American Psychologist,* 1975, *30,* 469–486.

The author, a prominent social psychologist, cautions readers that knowledgeable persons may use technology derived from experimental social psychology to manipulate and control others. He notes that many of these social psychology strategies work only when the manipulation is covert and secret, and he implicitly raises some ethical concerns.

BEECHER, H. K. "Ethics and Clinical Research." *New England Journal of Medicine,* 1966, *274,* 1354–1360.

This classic article caused a great stir when first published. The author describes in detail twenty-two examples of unethical or questionably ethical studies in experimental medicine, in most of which the researchers risked the health or the life of the subjects. He concludes that data unethically obtained should not be published and that more careful efforts should be made to obtain informed consent.

BERNSTEIN, J. E. "Ethical Considerations in Human Experimentation." *Journal of Clinical Pharmacology,* 1975, *15,* 579–590.

A relatively brief but thorough overview of the issues surrounding the ethics of research with humans, including a review of the historical development of ethical concerns and a discussion of the role of peer review committees.

BERSOFF, D. N. "Professional Ethics and Legal Responsibilities: On the Horns of a Dilemma." *Journal of School Psychology,* 1975, *13,* 359–376.

Although this article is devoted mainly to a discussion of the special ethical problems of school psychologists, it concludes with a trenchant critique of professional codes of ethics that is applicable to all the human services professions. The author contends that ethics codes are developed from the professional group's point of view and thus rarely reflect the values of the consumers of the professionals' services, that ethical principles are too abstract to be more than a general guide to actual behavior, and that enforcement practice limits the dissemination of any developing case material. Ethics codes may be but hollow symbols of a myth of professionalism, he says.

DEBAKEY, M. F. "Medical Research and the Golden Rule." *Journal of the American Medical Association,* 1968, *203,* 574–576.

In a brief note on medical ethics, this well-known surgeon concludes that ethical decisions in medicine must depend on the wisdom, integrity, and self-imposed restraints of the physician-scientist and his (sic) peers. The finest basis for ethical practice is the physician's personal credo based on general ethical norms and love and reverence for humanity. He opposes "control by association," formal laws, or rules, on the grounds that such regulation tends to be developed by persons with biased opinions and limited knowledge of science.

ROTH, L. H., MEISEL, A., and LIDZ, C. W. "Tests of Competency to Consent to Treatment." *American Journal of Psychiatry,* 1977, *134,* 279–284.

Various tests of competency to consent to treatment are described, and case examples are given. The authors note that, although in theory competency is an independent variable that determines whether the patient's decision about participating in treatment will be honored, in practice competency seems to be dependent on the interplay of the risk-benefit ratio of treatment and whether the patient consents. The more favorable the risk-benefit ratio for the proposed treatment, the more likely it is that a patient refusing that treatment will be judged incompetent and the more rigorous will be the test that is used to evaluate the patient's competence. In the authors' opinion, judgments of competency reflect social considerations and societal biases.

SCHWITZGEBEL, R. K. "A Contractual Model for the Protection of the Rights of Institutionalized Mental Patients." *American Psychologist,* 1975, *30,* 815–820.

The author conceptualizes treatment as a contractual activity in which the outcomes are specified in advance, with explicit contingencies for success or failure. He argues against the use of consent procedures in therapy, on the grounds that their use implies that the therapist may be doing something presumed to be harmful or wrong, or consent would not be necessary. As an alternative to consent, he recommends contracts and the protection of contract law. A major problem in obtaining consent, however, is the influence on the client's behavior that the professional is able to exert; the same influence and potential coercion would presumably be present when a contract is negotiated.

References

AGRAS, W. S. "Toward the Certification of Behavior Therapists?" *Journal of Applied Behavior Analysis,* 1973, *6,* 167–171.

American Institutes for Research. *Counter-Insurgency in Thailand: A Research and Development Proposal Submitted to the Advanced Research Projects Agency.* Pittsburgh: American Institutes for Research, 1976.

American Psychological Association. *Psychology as a Profession.* Washington, D.C.: American Psychological Association, 1968.

American Psychological Association. *Ethical Principles in the Conduct of Research with Human Participants.* Washington, D.C.: American Psychological Association, 1973.

American Psychological Association. *Standards for Educational and Psychological Tests.* Washington, D.C.: American Psychological Association, 1974.

References

American Psychological Association. *Ethical Standards of Psychologists: 1977 Revision.* Washington, D.C.: American Psychological Association, 1977a.

American Psychological Association. *Standards for Providers of Psychological Services.* Washington, D.C.: American Psychological Association, 1977b.

AXELROD, S. "Comparison of Individual and Group Contingencies in Two Special Classes." *Behavior Therapy,* 1973, *4,* 83–90.

AYLLON, T., and AZRIN, N. H. "The Measurement and Reinforcement of Behavior of Psychotics." *Journal of the Experimental Analysis of Behavior,* 1965, *8,* 357–383.

AYLLON, T., and AZRIN, N. H. *The Token Economy.* New York: Appleton-Century-Crofts, 1968.

BAER, D. M., WOLF, M. M., and RISLEY, T. R. "Some Current Dimensions of Applied Behavior Analysis." *Journal of Applied Behavior Analysis,* 1968, *1,* 91–97.

BANDURA, A. *Principles of Behavior Modification.* New York: Holt, Rinehart and Winston, 1969.

BANDURA, A. "Behavior Theory and the Models of Man." *American Psychologist,* 1974, *29,* 859–869.

BARBER, B., LALLY, J. J., MAKARUSHKA, J. L., and SULLIVAN, D. *Research on Human Subjects.* New York: Russell Sage, 1973.

BAZELON, D. L. "Psychologists in Corrections—Are They Doing Good for the Offender or Well for Themselves?" In S. L. Brodsky (Ed.), *Psychologists in the Criminal Justice System.* Chicago: University of Illinois Press, 1973.

BEECHER, H. K. "Ethics and Clinical Research." *New England Journal of Medicine,* 1966, *274,* 1354–1360.

BEGELMAN, D. A. "Ethical and Legal Issues of Behavior Modification." In M. Hersen, R. M. Eisler, and P. H. Miller (Eds.), *Progress in Behavior Modification.* Vol. 1. New York: Academic Press, 1975.

BERNSTEIN, J. E. "Ethical Considerations in Human Experimentation." *Journal of Clinical Pharmacology,* 1975, *15,* 579–590.

BIJOU, S. W. (Chair). "Legal and Ethical Problems in Behavior Modification: Case Study Approach." Symposium presented at the meeting of the American Psychological Association, Chicago, 1975.

BIJOU, S. W. (Chair). "Open Meeting: American Psychological Association Commission on Behavior Modification." Held at the meeting of the American Psychological Association, Washington, D.C., 1976.

BIJOU, S. W., and BAER, D. M. *Child Development: A Systematic and Empirical Theory.* Vol. 1. New York: Appleton-Century-Crofts, 1961.

BIJOU, S. W., PETERSON, R. F., HARRIS, F. R., ALLEN, K. E., and JOHNSTON, M. S. "Methodology for Experimental Studies of Young Children in Natural Settings." *Psychological Record,* 1969, *19,* 177–210.

BIRK, L., STOLZ, S. B., BRADY, J. P., BRADY, J. V., LAZARUS, A. A., LYNCH, J. J., ROSENTHAL, A. J., SKELTON, W. D., STEVENS, J. B., and THOMAS, E. J. *Behavior Therapy in Psychiatry.* Washington, D.C.: American Psychiatric Association, 1973.

BOOTZIN, R. R. *Behavior Modification and Therapy: An Introduction.* Cambridge, Mass.: Winthrop, 1975.

BROWN, B. S. "Behavior Modification: What It Is—and Isn't." *Today's Education,* January-February, 1976, pp. 67–69.

BROWN, B. S., WIENCKOWSKI, L. A., and STOLZ, S. B. *Behavior Modification: Perspective on a Current Issue.* DHEW Publication No. (ADM)75-202. Washington, D.C.: U.S. Government Printing Office, 1975.

BUDD, K. S., and BAER, D. M. "Behavior Modification and the Law: Implications of Recent Judicial Decisions." *Journal of Psychiatry & Law,* 1976, *4,* 171–244.

BURGESS, R. L. "A Bio-Behavioral Approach to the Analysis and Treatment of Environmental Problems: Population Growth, Resource Use, and Social Conflict." Paper presented at the 6th International Symposium on Behavior Modification, Panama City, Panama, 1976.

BURGESS, R. L., CLARK, R. N., and HENDEE, J. C. "An Experimental Analysis of Anti-Litter Procedures." *Journal of Applied Behavior Analysis,* 1971, *4,* 71–76.

References

BURTON, S. J. "The New Biotechnology and the Role of Legal Intervention." *American Journal of Orthopsychiatry,* 1974, *44,* 688–696.

BUSHELL, D., WROBEL, P. A., and MICHAELIS, M. L. "Applying 'Group' Contingencies to the Classroom Study Behavior of Preschool Children." *Journal of Applied Behavior Analysis,* 1968, *1,* 55–61.

CARRERA, F., III, and ADAMS, P. L. "An Ethical Perspective on Operant Conditioning." *Journal of the American Academy of Child Psychiatry,* 1970, *9,* 607–623.

CHAPMAN, C., and RISLEY, T. R. "Anti-Litter Procedures in an Urban High-Density Area." *Journal of Applied Behavior Analysis,* 1974, *7,* 377–384.

CHRISTY, P. R. "Does the Use of Tangible Rewards with Individual Children Affect Peer Observers?" *Journal of Applied Behavior Analysis,* 1975, *8,* 187–196.

COOKE, R. A., and TANNENBAUM, A. S. *The Performance of Institutional Review Boards.* Ann Arbor: Survey Research Center, Institute for Social Research, University of Michigan, 1977.

CORSINI, R. (Ed.). *Current Psychotherapies.* Itasca, Ill.: Peacock, 1973.

CRANBERG, L. "Ethical Code for Scientists?" *Science,* 1963, *141,* 1242.

CURRAN, W. J. "Governmental Regulation of the Use of Human Subjects in Medical Research: The Approach of Two Federal Agencies." In P. A. Freund (Ed.), *Experimentation with Human Subjects.* New York: Braziller, 1969.

DAVISON, G. C. "Countercontrol in Behavior Modification." In L. A. Hamerlynck, L. C. Handy, and E. J. Mash (Eds.), *Behavior Change: Methodology, Concepts, and Practice.* Champaign, Ill.: Research Press, 1973.

DAVISON, G. C. "Homosexuality: The Ethical Challenge." *Journal of Consulting and Clinical Psychology,* 1976, *44,* 157–162.

DAVISON, G. C., and STUART, R. B. "Behavior Therapy and Civil Liberties." *American Psychologist,* 1975, *30,* 755–763.

DOLLARD, J., and MILLER, N. E. *Personality and Psychotherapy.* New York: McGraw-Hill, 1950.

DRABMAN, R. S., SPITALNIK, R., and SPITALNIK, K. "Sociometric and

Disruptive Behavior as a Function of Four Types of Token Reinforcement Programs." *Journal of Applied Behavior Analysis,* 1974, *7,* 93–101.

DRABMAN, R. S., and TUCKER, R. D. "Why Classroom Token Economies Fail." *Journal of School Psychology,* 1974, *12,* 178–188.

EVERETT, P. B. "Application of Behavior Principles to Urban Transportation Problems." Paper presented at the meeting of the Midwestern Association of Behavior Analysis, Chicago, 1976.

EVERETT, P. B., HAYWARD, S. C., and MEYERS, A. W. "The Effects of a Token Reinforcement Procedure on Bus Riding." *Journal of Applied Behavior Analysis,* 1974, *7,* 1–10.

EYSENCK, H. J. *Behaviour Therapy and the Neuroses.* London: Pergamon, 1960.

EYSENCK, H. J. (Ed.). *Experiments in Behaviour Therapy.* New York: Pergamon, 1964.

FEINGOLD, B. D., and MAHONEY, M. J. "Reinforcement Effects on Intrinsic Interest: Undermining the Overjustification Hypothesis." *Behavior Therapy,* 1975, *6,* 367–377.

FILIPCZAK, J., and FRIEDMAN, R. M. "Some Controls on Applied Research in a Public Secondary School." In T. A. Brigham and A. C. Catania (Eds.), *Handbook of Applied Behavior Research: Social and Instructional Processes.* New York: Irvington-Neiburg/Wiley, in press.

FILIPCZAK, J., REESE, S., FENNELL, S., BASS, G., KENT, T., and GILMORE, S. *Progress Report: The PREP Project, Urban Junior High School.* Silver Spring, Md.: Institute for Behavioral Research, 1976.

FORD, J., and FOSTER, S. "Extrinsic Incentives and Token-Based Programs: A Reevaluation." *American Psychologist,* 1976, *31,* 87–90.

FOXX, R. M. "A Behavioral Approach to Gasoline Conservation." Paper presented at the meeting of the Midwestern Association of Behavioral Analysis, Chicago, 1976.

FRANK, J. D. (Chair). "Final Report of the American Psychological Association Commission on Behavior Modification." Symposium presented at the meeting of the Association for the Advancement of Behavior Therapy, New York City, 1976.

FRIEDMAN, P. R. "Legal Regulation of Applied Behavior Analysis in Mental Institutions and Prisons." *Arizona Law Review,* 1975, *17,* 39–104.

GELFAND, D. M., and HARTMANN, D. P. *Child Behavior Analysis and Therapy.* New York: Pergamon, 1975.

GITTELMAN, M. (Chair). "The Implications and Ethics of Behavior Modification Programs in the Treatment and Education of Children." Symposium presented at the meeting of the American Orthopsychiatric Association, Washington, D.C., 1975.

GLASER, D. *The Effectiveness of a Prison and Parole System.* Indianapolis: Bobbs-Merrill, 1964.

GOLDIAMOND, I. "Justified and Unjustified Alarm over Behavioral Control." In O. Milton and R. G. Wahler (Eds.), *Behavior Disorders: Perspectives and Trends.* 2nd ed. New York: Lippincott, 1969.

GOLDIAMOND, I. "Toward a Constructional Approach to Social Problems." *Behaviorism,* 1974, *2,* 1–84.

GOLDIAMOND, I. "Singling Out Behavior Modification for Legal Regulation: Some Effects on Patient Care, Psychotherapy, and Research in General." *Arizona Law Review,* 1975, *17,* 105–126.

GOLDIAMOND, I. "Singling out Self-Administered Behavior Therapies for Professional Overview: A Comment on Rosen." *American Psychologist,* 1976, *31,* 142–147.

GRAY, B. H. *Human Subjects in Medical Experimentation.* New York: Wiley, 1975.

HARRIS, V. W., BUSHELL, D., SHERMAN, J. A., and KANE, J. F. "Instructions, Feedback, Praise, Bonus Payments, and Teacher Behavior." *Journal of Applied Behavior Analysis,* 1975, *8,* 462.

HELDMAN, A. W. "Social Psychology versus the First Amendment Freedoms, Due Process Liberty, and Limited Government." *Cumberland-Samford Law Review,* 1973, *4,* 1–40.

HOBBS, T. R., and HOLT, M. M. "The Effects of Token Reinforcement on the Behavior of Delinquents in Cottage Settings." *Journal of Applied Behavior Analysis,* 1976, *9,* 189–198.

HOLLAND, J. G. "Behavior Modification for Prisoners, Patients, and Other People as a Prescription for the Planned Society." *Mexican Journal of the Analysis of Behavior,* 1975, *1,* 81–95.

HOLLAND, J. G. "Behaviorism: Part of the Problem or Part of the Solution?" *Journal of Applied Behavior Analysis,* in press.

KANTOR, J. R. *The Scientific Evolution of Psychology.* Vol. 2. Chicago: Principia, 1969.

KATZ, J. *Experimentation with Human Beings.* New York: Russell Sage, 1972.

KAZDIN, A. E. *Behavior Modification in Applied Settings.* Homewood, Ill.: Dorsey, 1975.

KENNEDY, R. E. "Behavior Modification in Prisons." In W. E. Craighead, A. E. Kazdin, and M. J. Mahoney (Eds.), *Behavior Modification: Principles, Issues and Applications.* Boston: Houghton-Mifflin, 1976.

KOHLENBERG, R., PHILLIPS, J., and PROCTOR, W. "A Behavioral Analysis of Peaking in Residential Electrical-Energy Consumers." *Journal of Applied Behavior Analysis,* 1976, *9,* 13–18.

KRASNER, L. "The Behavioral Scientist and Social Responsibility: No Place to Hide." *Journal of Social Issues,* 1965, *21* (2), 9–30.

LEPPER, M. R., GREEN, D., and NISBETT, R. E. "Undermining Children's Intrinsic Interest with Extrinsic Rewards: A Test of the 'Overjustification Hypothesis.' " *Journal of Personality and Social Psychology,* 1973, *28,* 129–137.

LEVINE, F. M., and FASNACHT, G. "Token Rewards May Lead to Token Learning." *American Psychologist,* 1974, *29,* 816–820.

LITOW, L., and PUMROY, D. K. "A Brief Review of Classroom Group-Oriented Contingencies." *Journal of Applied Behavior Analysis,* 1975, *8,* 341–347.

MAHONEY, M. J. *Cognition and Behavior Modification.* Cambridge, Mass.: Ballinger, 1974.

MALEY, R. F., and HAYES, S. C. "Coercion and Control: Ethical and Legal Issues." Paper presented at the conference on Behavior Analysis and Ethics, Morgantown, W. Va., June 1975.

MARTIN, R. "Ethical and Legal Implications of Behavior Modification in the Classroom." Paper delivered at the 1st annual Conference on School Psychology, Temple University, Philadelphia, June 1972.

MARTIN, R. *Behavior Modification: Human Rights and Legal Responsibilities.* Champaign, Ill.: Research Press, 1974.

MARTIN, R. *Legal Challenges to Behavior Modification.* Champaign, Ill.: Research Press, 1975.

MAY, J. G., RISLEY, T. R., TWARDOSZ, S., FRIEDMAN, P., BIJOU, S. W., WEXLER, D., and others. "Guidelines for the Use of Behavioral Procedures in State Programs for Retarded Persons." *M. R. Research,* 1975, *1* (1, entire issue).

Medical Research Council. "Responsibility in Investigations on Human Subjects: Statement by Medical Research Council." *British Medical Journal,* 1964, *2,* 178–180.

MILAN, M. A., and MCKEE, J. M. "The Cellblock Token Economy: Token Reinforcement Procedures in a Maximum Security Correctional Institution for Adult Male Felons." *Journal of Applied Behavior Analysis,* 1976, *9,* 253–275.

MILAN, M. A., WOOD, L. F., WILLIAMS, R. L., ROGERS, J. G., HAMPTON, L. R., and MCKEE, J. M. *Applied Behavior Analysis and the Imprisoned Adult Felon. Project I: The Cellblock Token Economy.* Montgomery, Ala.: Rehabilitation Research Foundation, 1974.

National Commission for the Protection of Human Subjects of Biomedical and Behavioral Research. *Report and Recommendations: Research Involving Prisoners.* DHEW Publication No. (OS) 76–131. Washington, D.C.: U.S. Government Printing Office, 1976.

"New Tool: Reinforcement for Good Work." *Business Week,* December 18, 1971, pp. 76–77.

O'LEARY, K. D. "Behavior Modification in the Classroom: A Rejoinder to Winett and Winkler." *Journal of Applied Behavior Analysis,* 1972, *5,* 592–601.

O'LEARY, K. D., BECKER, W. C., EVANS, M. B., and SAUDARGAS, R. A. "A Token Reinforcement Program in a Public School: A

Replication and Systematic Analysis." *Journal of Applied Behavior Analysis,* 1969, *2,* 3–13.

O'LEARY, K. D., and DRABMAN, R. S. "Token Reinforcement Programs in the Classroom: A Review." *Psychological Bulletin,* 1971, *75,* 379–398.

O'LEARY, K. D., and O'LEARY, S. G. *Classroom Management: The Successful Use of Behavior Modification.* New York: Pergamon, 1972.

O'LEARY, S. G., and O'LEARY, K. D. "Behavior Modification in the School." In H. Leitenberg (Ed.), *Handbook of Behavior Modification.* Englewood Cliffs, N.J.: Prentice-Hall, 1976.

OPTON, E. M., JR. "Psychiatric Violence Against Prisoners: When Therapy Is Punishment." *Mississippi Law Journal,* 1974, *45,* 605–644.

OPTON, E. M., JR. "Institutional Behavior Modification as a Fraud and Sham." *Arizona Law Review,* 1975, *17,* 20–28.

POWERS, R. B., OSBORNE, J. G., and ANDERSON, E. G. "Positive Reinforcement of Litter Removal in the Natural Environment." *Journal of Applied Behavior Analysis,* 1973, *6,* 579–586.

REIMRINGER, M. J., MORGAN, S. W., and BRAMWELL, P. F. "Succinylcholine as a Modifier of Acting-Out Behavior." *Clinical Medicine,* 1970, *77* (7), 28–29.

RISLEY, T. R. "Certify Procedures not People." In W. S. Wood (Ed.), *Issues in Evaluating Behavior Modification.* Champaign, Ill.: Research Press, 1975.

ROLLINS, H. A., MCCANDLESS, B. R., THOMPSON, M., and BRASSELL, W. R. "Project Success Environment: An Extended Application of Contingency Management in Inner-City Schools." *Journal of Educational Psychology,* 1974, *66,* 167–178.

ROOS, P. "Human Rights and Behavior Modification." *Mental Retardation,* 1974, *12* (3), 3–6.

SCHWITZGEBEL, R. K. "A Contractual Model for the Protection of the Rights of Institutionalized Mental Patients." *American Psychologist,* 1975, *30,* 815–820.

SEAVER, W. B., and PATTERSON, A. H. "Decreasing Fuel-Oil Consumption Through Feedback and Social Commendation." *Journal of Applied Behavior Analysis,* 1976, *9,* 147–152.

Selective Service Orientation Kit. Chief, Public Information, Selective Service System (National Headquarters), 1965.

SERBER, M., and KEITH, C. G. "The Atascadero Project: Model of a Sexual Retraining Program for Incarcerated Homosexual Pedophiles." *Journal of Homosexuality,* 1974, *1,* 87–97.

SHAPIRO, D., and BIRK, L. "Group Therapy in Experimental Perspective." *International Journal of Group Psychotherapy,* 1967, *17,* 211–224.

SHAW, M. "Ethical Implications of a Behavioural Approach." In D. Jehu, P. Hardiker, M. Yelloly, and M. Shaw. *Behaviour Modification in Social Work.* London: Wiley, 1972.

SHERMAN, A. R. *Behavior Modification: Theory and Practice.* Belmont, Calif.: Wadsworth, 1973.

SKINNER, B. F. *The Behavior of Organisms.* New York: Appleton-Century-Crofts, 1938.

SKINNER, B. F. *Science and Human Behavior.* New York: Macmillan, 1953.

SKINNER, B. F. *Verbal Behavior.* New York: Appleton-Century-Crofts, 1957.

SKINNER, B. F. *Cumulative Record.* (rev. ed.) New York: Appleton-Century-Crofts, 1961.

SKINNER, B. F. *The Technology of Teaching.* New York: Appleton-Century-Crofts, 1968.

SKINNER, B. F. *Contingencies of Reinforcement: A Theoretical Analysis.* New York: Appleton-Century-Crofts, 1969.

SKINNER, B. F. *Beyond Freedom and Dignity.* New York: Knopf, 1971.

STOKES, T. F., and BAER, D. M. "An Implicit Technology of Generalization." *Journal of Applied Behavior Analysis,* 1977, *10,* 349–367.

STOLZ, S. B. "Evaluation of Therapeutic Efficacy of Behavior Modification in a Community Setting." *Behaviour Research and Therapy,* 1976, *14,* 479–481.

STOLZ, S. B. "Why No Guidelines for Behavior Modification?" *Journal of Applied Behavior Analysis,* 1977, *10,* 541–547.

STOLZ, S. B. "Ethics of Social and Educational Interventions: Historical Context and a Behavioral Analysis." In T. A. Brigham and A. C. Catania (Eds.), *Handbook of Applied Behavior Research: Social and Instructional Processes.* New York: Irvington-Neiburg/Wiley, in press, a.

STOLZ, S. B. "Ethical Issues in Behavior Modification." In G. Bermant and H. Kelman (Eds.), *Ethics of Social Intervention.* Washington, D.C.: Hemisphere Publications, in press, b.

STOLZ, S. B., WIENCKOWSKI, L. A., and BROWN, B. S. "Behavior Modification: A Perspective on Critical Issues." *American Psychologist,* 1975, *30,* 1027–1048.

STRAIN, P. S., SHORES, R. E., and KERR, M. M. "An Experimental Analysis of 'Spillover' Effects on the Social Interaction of Behaviorally Handicapped Preschool Children." *Journal of Applied Behavior Analysis,* 1976, *9,* 31–40.

STUART, R. B. "Notes on the Ethics of Behavior Research and Intervention." In L. A. Hamerlynck, L. C. Handy, and E. J. Mash (Eds.), *Behavior Change: Methodology, Concepts, and Practice.* Champaign, Ill.: Research Press, 1973.

SULZER-AZAROFF, B., THAW, J., and THOMAS, C. "Behavioral Competencies for the Evaluation of Behavior Modifiers." In W. S. Wood (Ed.), *Issues in Evaluating Behavior Modification.* Champaign, Ill.: Research Press, 1975.

U.S. Congress, House, Committee on the Judiciary, Subcommittee on Courts, Civil Liberties, and the Administration of Justice. *Oversight Hearing: Behavior Modification Programs in the Federal Bureau of Prisons.* 93rd Cong., 2d sess., 27 February 1974 (Serial No. 26). Washington, D.C.: U.S. Government Printing Office, 1974a.

U.S. Congress, Senate, Committee on the Judiciary, Subcommittee on Constitutional Rights. *Individual Rights and the Federal Role in Behavior Modification.* 93rd Cong., 2d sess., November 1974. Washington, D.C.: U.S. Government Printing Office, 1974b.

WALTERS, H. C. *Military Psychology: Its Use in Modern War and Indirect Conflict.* Dubuque, Iowa: Brown, 1968.

WEXLER, D. B. "Token and Taboo: Behavior Modification, Token

Economies, and the Law." *California Law Review,* 1973, *61,* 81–109.

WEXLER, D. B. "Reflections on the Legal Regulation of Behavior Modification in Institutional Settings." *Arizona Law Review,* 1975, *17,* 132–143.

WILSON, G. T., and EVANS, I. M. "The Therapist-Client Relationship in Behavior Therapy." In A. Gurman and A. Razin (Eds.), *The Therapist's Contribution to Effective Psychotherapy.* New York: Pergamon Press, in press.

WINETT, R. A., and WINKLER, R. C. "Current Behavior Modification in the Classroom: Be Still, Be Quiet, Be Docile." *Journal of Applied Behavior Analysis,* 1972, *5,* 499–504.

WITMER, J. F., and GELLER, E. S. "Facilitating Paper Recycling: Effects of Prompts, Raffles, and Contests." *Journal of Applied Behavior Analysis,* 1976, *9,* 315–322.

WOLF, M. M. "Social Validity: The Case for Subjective Measurement or How Applied Behavior Analysis Is Finding Its Heart." *Journal of Applied Behavior Analysis,* in press.

WOLFENSBERGER, W. "Ethical Issues in Research with Human Subjects." *Science,* 1967, *155,* 47–51.

WOLPE, J. *Psychotherapy by Reciprocal Inhibition.* Stanford, Calif.: Stanford University Press, 1958.

WOLPE, J. "Psychotherapy by Reciprocal Inhibition." *Conditioned Reflex,* 1968, *3,* 234–240.

WOLPE, J. *The Practice of Behavior Therapy.* New York: Pergamon, 1969a.

WOLPE, J. "Basic Principles and Practices of Behavior Therapy of Neuroses." *American Journal of Psychiatry,* 1969b, *125,* 1242–1247.

WOLPE, J. "How Can 'Cognitions' Influence Desensitization?" *Behaviour Research and Therapy,* 1969c, *7,* 219.

World Medical Association. "Human Experimentation: Code of Ethics of the World Medical Association." *British Medical Journal,* 1964, *2,* 177.

Index

A

Accountability: issue of, 25–27, 111; in out-patient settings, 38–39; in prisons, 65–66; references on, 169, 175; in schools, 56–57; standards for, 149–152, 160–162
ADAMS, P. L., 10, 167, 186
AGRAS, W. S., 27, 104, 183
ALLEN, K. E., 32, 185
American Civil Liberties Union Foundation, National Prison Project of, 12
American Institutes for Research, 93, 183
American Psychiatric Association, xvi, 14–15; Task Force on Behavior Therapy of, 15
American Psychological Association (APA), xi–xii, xvi, 2, 8, 13, 16, 104, 107–109, 114, 115–131, 133–163, 183–184; Board of Professional Affairs of, xvii; Board of Social and Ethical Responsibility of, xii; Commission on Behavior Modification of, xii–xvii, 15–16, 17, 34; Committee on Scientific and Professional Ethics and Conduct (CSPEC) of, 115–116; Committee on Standards for Providers of Psychological Services of, 133–134
ANDERSON, E. G., 92, 191
Applied behavior analysis, 2–3
ARGYRIS, C., 178–179
Armstrong v. *Bensinger,* 176
Association for Advancement of Behavior Therapy (AABT), xvi, 15, 102, 108*n*
Associations, professional, and ethical issues, 8, 14–15
Aversive controls: criticism of, 102; issue of, 24–25; in prisons, 65, 78; references on, 169, 175
AXELROD, S., 53, 184
AYLLON, T., 41, 184
AZRIN, N. H., 41, 184

B

BAER, D. M., 6, 28, 32, 44, 74, 171–172, 184, 185, 192
BANDURA, A., ix–x, xii, 10, 20, 165–166, 184
BARBER, B., 7, 8, 106, 184
BARRON, J., 134
BASS, G., 50, 187
BAZELON, D. L., 88–89, 184
BECKER, W. C., 23–24, 190–191
BEECHER, H. K., 106, 179, 184
BEGELMAN, D. A., 105, 184
Behavior modification: characteristics of, 3–5; context of, 1–16; criticisms of, 8–12, 101–103, 166–167, 168–169, 173; defined, 1, 2–5; ethics of, references on, 165–171, 178–181; history of, 5–6; in institutions, 41–46; issues in, xiv–xv, 17–34, 110–114; in out-patient settings, 35–39; in prisons, 58–89; recommendations on, 101–114; in schools, 47–58; in society, 91–100; society's concerns about, 12–15; techniques in, 5; terms in, 2–5, 11
Behavior therapy, 2
BERNSTEIN, J. E., 7, 179, 184
BERSOFF, D. N., 179
BIJOU, S. W., xii, xiv, xv, xvi, 6, 23, 32, 184–185, 190

Index

BIRK, L., 10, 15, 185, 192
BLUM, M. L., 153
BOOTZIN, R. R., 5, 185
BOUHOUTSOS, J. C., 133, 153
BRAMWELL, P. F., 102, 191
BRASSELL, W. R., 28, 50, 56–57, 191
BROWN, B. S., 14, 56, 102, 166, 185, 193
BRUCH, H., 166–167
BUDD, K. S., 44, 171–172, 185
Bureau of Prisons, 175–176, 178
BURGESS, R. L., 92, 185
BURTON, S. J., 30, 186
BUSHELL, D., 52, 56, 186, 188

C

CARON, P., 170
CARRERA, F., III, 10, 167, 186
CENTOR, A., 133, 134, 153
CHAPMAN, C., 92, 186
CHRISTY, P. R., 55, 186
CLARK, J. H., 133, 153
CLARK, R. N., 92, 185
Client, identification of: concepts of, 18–21; in institutions, 42; in out-patient settings, 36–37; in prisons, 60, 81–83; in schools, 48–49; in society, 95–96
Client's rights, protection of: in institutions, 43–46; issues in, 29–31, 112–113; in prisons, 67–71; references on, 168–169, 170, 172; in schools, 57–58; in society, 96–98; standards on, 123–124, 144–145, 158
Clonce v. *Richardson,* 171, 173–174
Confidentiality and record keeping: issues in, 28–29, 112; in prisons, 66–67; standards on, 122–123, 148–149
Congress, and behavior modification, 12–14
Contingencies Applicable to Special Education (CASE), 168
COOKE, R. A., 8, 186
CORSINI, R., 24, 25, 186
Countercontrol: concept of, 19–20, 171; in out-patient settings, 37; in prisons, 72; in schools, 48
Court decisions: and behavior modification, 12; on confidentiality, 29; on due process in prisons, 68; on informed consent, 44; and intervention methods, 22–23; on punishment in prisons, 69–70; references on, 166, 171–175, 176
CRANBERG, L., 8, 186
CURRAN, W. J., 7, 186

D

DAVISON, G. C., 20, 31, 105, 186
DEBAKEY, M. F., 180
Declaration of Helsinki, 7
Department of Health, Education, and Welfare (DHEW), 7; National Advisory Council for the Protection of Human Subjects of, 14
DOLLARD, J., 6, 186
Donaldson v. *O'Connor,* 173
DRABMAN, R. S., 52, 53, 56, 186–187, 191
Draper Correctional Center, 177
Due process: in prisons, 68; references on, 175

E

EDGERTON, H. A., 153
Emery Air Freight, 168
ERICKSON, R. C., 167
ERVIN, S. J., JR., 13, 171
Ethical issues: checklist of, 108–114; government regulations on, 7–8; history of, 6–8; in institutions, 41–46; international codes on, 7; of interventions, 17–34; in out-patient settings, 35–39; in prisons, 59–72; professional associations and, 8, 14–15; references on, 165–

Index

171, 178–181; in schools, 47–58; in society, 91–100
Evaluation: of psychologists, 27–28, 66; standards for, 151, 161–162
EVANS, I. M., 20, 194
EVANS, M. B., 23–24, 190–191
EVERETT, P. B., 92, 187
EYSENCK, H. J., 6, 187

F

FASNACHT, G., 54, 189
FEINGOLD, B. D., 54, 187
FENNELL, S., 50, 187
FILIPCZAK, J., 50, 57, 187
FORD, J., 54, 187
FOSTER, S., 54, 187
FOXX, R. M., 92, 187
FRANK, J. D., xii–xiii, xv, xvi, 187
FRIEDLANDER, F., 134
FRIEDMAN, P. R., xiii, xv, 23, 29, 30, 45, 68, 70, 172–173, 188, 190
FRIEDMAN, R. M., 57, 187

G

GELFAND, D. M., 5, 188
GELLER, E. S., 92, 194
GILMORE, S., 50, 187
GITTELMAN, M., xvi, 188
GLASER, D., 87, 188
Goals, selection of. *See* Problem, definition of, and selection of goals
GOLDBERGER, D., 176
GOLDIAMOND, I., 30–31, 104, 172–173, 188
GRAY, B. H., 7, 106, 188
GREEN, D., 53, 189
Group comparison design, 33–34
Group-oriented reinforcement programs, 52–53
Guidelines for behavior modification: alternatives to, 106–110; disadvantages of, 104–106; need for, 101–103; range of, 103–104
GUREL, B., 116

H

HALL, L., 133
HALL, M. D., 133, 134, 153
HALLECK, S. L., 168
HAMPTON, L. R., 75, 82, 190
HARRIS, F. R., 32, 185
HARRIS, V. W., 56, 188
HARTMANN, D. P., 5, 188
HAYES, S. C., 22–23, 31, 189
HAYWARD, S. C., 92, 187
HELDMAN, A. W., 9, 173, 188
HENDEE, J. C., 92, 185
HENLE, M., 133
HOBBS, N., xiii, 162, 163
HOBBS, T. R., 82, 176–177, 188
HOLLAND, J. G., xiii, xv, 63, 64, 78, 99, 106, 168–169, 189
HOLT, M. M., 82, 176–177, 188
Home-based consequences, 51–52

I

Informed consent: and client's rights, 30–31; in institutions, 43–45; issues in, 113–114; in prisons, 67–68, 78–79; references on, 168, 169, 174, 175, 179, 180–181; in society, 97–98
Institutions: client identification in, 42; client's rights in, 43–46; ethical issues in, 41–46; intervention method in, 43; problem definition in, 42–43
Internal Revenue Service, 93
Intervention methods: hierarchical sequence of, 23–24; in institutions, 43; issues in selection of, 22–25, 111; in schools, 51–56
Interventions, psychological: and ethics, 2, 17–34; evaluation of, 27–28, 66; recommendation on, 107–108; right to terminate, 112, 114, 172, 173–

174; standards for, 143–149, 158–159

J

JACOBS, D. F., 133, 134, 153
JOHNSTON, M. S., 32, 185
Joint Commission on Accreditation of Hospitals (JCAH), 136

K

Kaimowitz v. *Department of Mental Health for the State of Michigan,* 44*n*, 171
KANE, J. F., 56, 188
KANTOR, J. R., 6, 189
KASSIRER, L. B., 173–174
KATZ, J., 6, 189
KAZDIN, A. E., 5, 189
KEITH, C. G., 105, 192
KENNEDY, R. E., 87, 177, 189
KENT, T., 50, 187
KERR, M. M., 55, 193
KIRK, B. A., 134
Knecht, 171
KOHLENBERG, R., 92, 189
KRASNER, L., xiii, xv, 31, 189

L

LACEY, H., xiii, xv
LALLY, J. J., 7, 8, 106, 184
Law Enforcement Assistance Administration (LEAA), xi, 13
LEPPER, M. R., 53, 189
LEVINE, F. M., 54, 189
LIDZ, C. W., 180
Litigation. *See* Court decisions
LITOW, L., 52, 53, 189
LONDON, P., 169

M

MCCANDLESS, B. R., 28, 50, 56–57, 191
MCKEE, J. M., 75, 82, 176–177, 190
MCMILLAN, J. J., 153
MAHONEY, M. J., 20, 54, 187, 189
MAKARUSHKA, J. L., 7, 8, 106, 184
MALEY, R. F., 22–23, 31, 189
MARTIN, R., 27, 30, 53, 56, 109, 174, 190
MARTINEZ, F. H., 153
MAY, J. G., 23, 190
Medical Research Council, 7, 190
MEISEL, A., 180
Mental Health Law Project, 12
MEYERS, A. W., 92, 187
MICHAELIS, M. L., 52, 186
MILAN, M. A., 75, 82, 176–177, 190
MILLER, N. E., 6, 186
MORGAN, S. W., 102, 191
Multiple-baseline design, 32–33
MUTHARD, J. E., 153

N

National Commission for the Protection of Human Subjects of Biomedical and Behavioral Research, xvi, 7–8, 14, 67, 169, 190
National Institute of Mental Health, 14, 136, 166
National Research Act (PL 93–348), 14
NISBETT, R. E., 53, 189
Nuremberg Code, 7, 8, 171

O

O'LEARY, K. D., 5, 23–24, 34, 47, 49–53, 55, 105, 169, 190–191
O'LEARY, S. G., 5, 34, 47, 50, 52, 55, 169, 191
OPTON, E. M., JR., 80, 102, 177–178, 191
OSBORNE, J. G., 92, 191
OSSORIO, A., 133
Out-patient settings: accountability in, 38–39; client identification in, 36–37; ethical issues in, 35–39; problem definition in, 37–38

Index

P

PACHT, A. R., 153
PAGE, S., 170
Paraprofessionals, evaluation of, 28
Patient advocate, and client's rights, 45–46
PATTERSON, A. H., 92, 191
Patuxent Institution, 176, 177
PETERSON, R. F., 32, 185
PHILLIPS, J., 92, 189
PIERCE, W. D., 153
POWERS, R. B., 92, 191
Prisoners: congressional concern about, 13; control of, 60–61, 62; rights of, 67–71
Prisons: accountability in, 65–66; behavior modification in, critique of, 73–89; client identification in, 60, 81–83; confidentiality in, 66–67; ethical issues in, 59–72; future of, 86–89; goals and assumptions in, 79–86; prisoners' rights in, 67–71; problem defining in, 60–62, 83–86; program implementation in, 74–79; quality of staff and intervention in, 66; references on, 175–179; and rehabilitation, 62, 74–76; research-oriented programs in, 64–65; total programs in, 62–64; "treatment" in, 76–77; treatment-oriented programs in, 65
Privacy, in prisons, 70
Problem, definition of, and selection of goals: in institutions, 42–43; issue of, 21–22, 110–111, 112; in out-patient settings, 37–38; in prisons, 60–62, 83–86; references on, 169, 170; in schools, 49–51; in society, 96
PROCTOR, W., 92, 189
Project Success Environment, 50, 56
Psychologists: and assessment techniques, 126–127; and client's rights, 123–124; competence of, 118–119; and confidentiality, 122–123; defined, 139–141, 153–156; dual alliance of, issues of, 112–113; ethical standards of, 115–131; evaluation of, 27–28, 66, 111; and institutional change, 98–100; moral and legal standards of, 119–120; professional relationships of, 124–126; public statements of, 120–122; and research, 128–130; responsibility of, 116–117; standards for, 115–163
PUMROY, D. K., 52, 53, 189
Punishment, in prisons, 68–70

R

Record keeping. *See* Confidentiality and record keeping
REESE, S., 50, 187
REIMRINGER, M. J., 102, 191
Research: on interventions in prisons, 61–62; issues in, 31–34; references on, 179, 180; standards on, 128–130
Reversal procedure, 31–32
RISLEY, T. R., 23, 27, 32, 92, 184, 186, 190, 191
ROGERS, J. G., 75, 82, 190
ROLLINS, H. A., 28, 50, 56–57, 191
ROOS, P., 26, 170, 191
ROTH, L. H., 180

S

SAUDARGAS, R. A., 23–24, 190–191
Schools: accountability in, 56–57; client identification in, 48–49; client's rights in, 57–58; ethical issues in, 47–58; intervention method in, 51–56; problem definition in, 49–51
SCHWITZGEBEL, R. K., 31, 180–181, 191
SEAVER, W. B., 92, 191

Index

Selective Service System, 93–95, 192
Senate Subcommittee on Constitutional Rights, 13–14
SERBER, M., 105, 192
SHAPIRO, D., 10, 192
SHAW, M., 106, 192
SHERMAN, A. R., 5, 192
SHERMAN, J. A., 56, 188
SHORES, R. E., 55, 193
SIMON, G. C., 153
SKINNER, B. F., 6, 9, 11, 21, 173, 192
SMITH, M. B., 134, 162, 163
Social validation, and accountability, 26
Society: behavior modification in, 92–95; client identification in, 95–96; client's rights in, 96–98; ethical issues in, 91–100; goal selection in, 96
SORENSON, W., 133
SPECE, R. G., JR., 174
Special Treatment and Rehabilitative Training (START), 13, 168, 171, 173–174, 177, 178
SPITALNIK, K., 52, 186–187
SPITALNIK, R., 52, 186–187
Standards: ethical, 115–131; history of, 135–137; principles and implications of, 137–139; for psychologists, 115–163
STIER, S., xiv
STOKES, T. F., 28, 74, 192
STOLZ, S. B., xiii, xv, xxi–xxii, 14, 15, 32, 78, 101*n*, 102, 106, 166, 170–171, 185, 192–193
STRAIN, P. S., 55, 193
STUART, R. B., 31, 33, 34, 186, 193
SULLIVAN, D., 7, 8, 106, 184
SULZER-AZAROFF, B., 27–28, 193

T

Tangible reinforcers: issues of, in schools, 54–56; side effects of, 53–54
TANNENBAUM, A. S., 8, 186
THAW, J., 27–28, 193
Therapy: control related to, 10; research in, 31–34. *See also* Treatment
THOMAS, C., 27–28, 193
THOMPSON, M., 28, 50, 56–57, 191
Treatment: in prisons, 70–71, 76–77; punishment distinguished from, 178; rights to, 70–71, 172, 173–174; social regulation distinguished from, x
TRYON, W. W., 174–175
TUCKER, R. D., 56, 187
TWARDOSZ, S., 23, 190

U

ULRICH, R., 171

V

Values: and definition of problem, 21–22; in prisons, 70; in schools, 50–51

W

WALTERS, H. C., 93, 193
WARREN, S. A., 153
WELLNER, A. M., 153
WEXLER, D., xiii, xv, 22, 23, 55, 76, 171, 175, 190, 193–194
WIENCKOWSKI, L. A., 14, 102, 166, 185, 193
WILLIAMS, R. L., 75, 82, 190
WILSON, G. T., xiii, xv, 20, 194
WINETT, R. A., 49–50, 194
WINKLER, R. C., 49–50, 194
WITMER, J. F., 92, 194
WOLF, M. M., 26, 32, 184, 194
WOLFENSBERGER, W., 8, 194
WOLPE, J., 6, 194
WOOD, L. F., 75, 82, 190
World Medical Association, 7, 194
WROBEL, P. A., 52, 186
Wyatt v. *Stickney,* 136, 171, 175

Y

YATES, E., 170